FAITH NOTES

A CHRIST-CENTERED **SURVIVAL KIT** FOR YOUNG WOMEN

Cassie Moore

CONCORDIA PUBLISHING HOUSE · SAINT LOUIS

DEDICATION

....

To all the young women I've been blessed to
work with throughout my career:
Your courage to authentically share your
passion, sorrow, and joy makes the world
(and me) better.

Published by Concordia Publishing House
3558 S. Jefferson Ave., St. Louis, MO 63118-3968
1-800-325-3040 • cph.org

Scripture quotations are from the ESV® Bible (The Holy Bible, English Standard Version®),
ccpyright © 2001 by Crossway, a publishing ministry of Good News Publishers. Used by
permission. All rights reserved.

Cover image © iStock.com

Manufactured in China

1 2 3 4 5 6 7 8 9 10   33 32 31 30 29 28 27 26 25 24

MY NAME IS:

....

I AM THANKFUL TO WALK IN FAITH
WITH JESUS, MY SAVIOR!

....

You opened this devotion book because you're curious, brave, and probably struggling with something. Welcome to the club. You're not alone.

Right now, you might be feeling a mix of emotions as you tackle life—everything from anxiety, fear, and shame to joy, excitement, and happiness. You might be in a tough season, and you might struggle with loneliness, confusion, or uncertainty. Or, you might be having a mountain-top experience and are filled with hope.

Every one of us is trying to learn who God made us to be and how to navigate the world. But the good news? God is right there with us as we try to figure it out.

By absorbing Scripture and focusing on the work of Jesus for you, you'll see the overwhelming love, security, and hope that comes from being a beloved child of God. That makes all the difference as you cope with life's challenges.

How can you use this devotional? Here are some tips:

☐ Read without distraction. A thousand things compete for our attention, but it benefits your brain and soul to step away and be still for a few minutes. Tuck your phone and computer away and treat yourself to me time to read and reflect on your faith life.

☐ Use the "Faith Notes" sections to journal, think, pray, doodle, and apply what you've read.

- ☐ Consider keeping a journal or a video blog, or talk to a friend or mentor about what you're reading.

- ☐ Go deeper by reading the whole chapter of a Bible passage that's shared or maybe even the entire book of the Bible the passage comes from. God speaks directly to our hearts through Scripture.

- ☐ Share what you're learning with a friend, sibling, parent, or trusted adult—maybe on a car ride to school or over a meal. This can help you better process and absorb what the Holy Spirit whispers in His Word.

- ☐ Don't worry about reading this book from front to back. Look at the table of contents, then choose a devotion that fits your situation and interest in the moment. Sometimes rereading the same devotion can be helpful too.

- ☐ Don't feel guilty if you don't read every day. It takes time to build healthy habits. Try setting an alarm for five minutes of time with God every day for a week, and spend time praying, reading your Bible, and reading devotions. Don't beat yourself up if you miss a day (or week or month!)—God's grace is there for you, no matter what.

Despite the unexpected twists and turns we face in life, one thing is certain: Christ loves us and offers us freedom through His sacrificial death on the cross. He comforts us in our trials and walks with us through every hardship, giving us the strength to face our journey through life with peace and confidence. Lean on Jesus, in the good times and bad. He is *always* there for you.

Let the adventure begin, my friend.

CONTENTS

SPIRITUAL LIFE

ANXIETY AND MENTAL HEALTH

PURITY

FAMILY AND HOME

HEALTH AND SELF

CHARACTER AND IDENTITY

1

Jeremiah 29:11–12
YOUR STORY

My grandma taught me to sew when I was a little girl. She was a pro, whipping up blankets and clothes with ease.

While I learned just the basics of how to hem or repair cloth, those sewing skills have served me well. I've carried a tiny sewing kit to many events, and you'd be shocked at how many times I've had to fix a button or a busted seam in a dress.

If you've ever tried to stitch something, you know that every thread matters. Even though they may be tiny and sometimes invisible in your clothing, stitches serve an important function to make something what it is.

In the same way, each experience in your life is a stitch in the grand tapestry of who you are. All those tiny threads weave together to make you unique and to serve as testament to God's design for your life.

The story of your life matters. But in a culture that idolizes comparison and conformity, it can be hard to believe that your unique story has a purpose.

The story of your life may be largely good. Perhaps you were baptized as a baby and grew up in church with a loving family always there to support you. What a testimony to God's faithfulness in your life!

Perhaps, though, you've just joined God's church after a life full of challenges. Maybe you had to hit rock bottom to realize that there's more to life than the emptiness that comes without Jesus at the center.

Or maybe you're still mulling over this whole faith thing, wondering if you want to know more.

Even if you have come to this point broken, reeling from pain and feeling messy, your story is testament to God's incredible grace.

In Jesus, we have a Savior who accepts us just as we are. It doesn't matter what we've been through or what decisions we've made or what our reputation is. He sees every ugly thought we've had, every mistake we've made, and all the painful moments we've endured—and He welcomes us with open arms.

Some people find it difficult to accept that Jesus gives us His love without expecting anything in return. It may be hard to hear that God is your heavenly Father and trust that He won't disappoint you or hurt you. But, truly, God has great plans for you.

Jeremiah 29:11–12 reminds us,

> For I know the plans I have for you, declares the
> LORD, plans for welfare and not for evil, to give you
> a future and a hope. Then you will call upon Me
> and come and pray to Me, and I will hear you.

Whatever your story may be and however you got here, you're a part of God's family now. He loves you completely, quirks and messy past and all. You are stitched together with Christ, forgiven by His cross, strengthened by His love, and supported by His grace. No matter what challenges you face in life, those threads holding you together will hold firm and keep you whole.

Faith Notes

....
....
....
....
....
....
....
....
....
....
....
....
....
....
....
....
....
....
....

2

2 Timothy 3:14–15; 2 Peter 3:18
GROWING UP

How often do you worry about your future?

If you're like most people, the answer is a lot. It doesn't matter what age you are because many of us worry about what's ahead. Even if things seem to be going fine, thinking about the future can induce fear, anxiety, and even panic.

Growing up is hard. It's natural to have concerns about facing something you've never faced before, whether that's navigating the middle school lunchroom, taking that AP calculus class, or moving away for college.

I find it helpful to look back and remember all the times I've faced something new and scary and realize how God guided me through. Sometimes it takes looking at the past to see how God provided encouraging friends, patient parents or siblings, caring coaches and teachers, or faithful pastors at just the right time.

The process of growing up requires trust in yourself and trust in your heavenly Father. He's given you a brain and a body that continue to grow and mature so you can face every new challenge. He's also given you the gift of Himself in the promise that He will always love you, care for you, and be with you. Faith in Him, which has been yours since you were baptized, equips you for the challenges God knows you will face in this life.

As 2 Timothy 3:14–15 reminds us,

> But as for you, continue in what you have learned and have firmly believed, knowing from whom you learned it and how from childhood you have been acquainted with the sacred writings, which are able to make you wise for salvation through faith in Christ Jesus.

Think of it this way: little first grade you would have freaked out trying to solve fifth grade math problems, right? Yet you progressed through first grade math, then second and third grade, and into fourth grade math. At the end of your fourth grade math classes, you had built up the brain power and knowledge to take the next step into fifth grade math.

Life is the same way. You're ready for each new step when you get there.

You see, God patiently prepares us for every moment we face in life. If you look too far ahead, you'll get freaked out. Yet when you look at His faithfulness through your whole life and remember how He has led you step-by-step as you've grown, you can face the future with confidence.

As 2 Peter 3:18 says,

> But grow in the grace and knowledge of our Lord and Savior Jesus Christ. To Him be the glory both now and to the day of eternity. Amen.

Growing up is hard. But the more you know about how the Holy Spirit works in your life to strengthen your faith in Jesus and to guide you along the path God has planned for you, the more you are ready for whatever next step you should take. Right now, all you need to do is grow in the grace and knowledge of Jesus, believing that God is right there with you as you step out.

Faith Notes

....
....
....
....
....
....
....
....
....
....
....
....
....
....
....
....
....
....

3

Romans 8:38–39
WHAT REALLY MATTERS

A few years ago, I was responsible for a major part of a massive youth conference. My team and I had worked for years to prepare for tens of thousands of people who would experience the event.

In the weeks leading up to the conference and during the frantic set up and operation period we carried out, immense stress was constant.

Some of my teammates became obsessed with controlling tiny details that didn't matter much. Others became withdrawn, so focused on work that they barely talked. Still others verged on reckless giddiness, pulling pranks and seeking ways to make everyone else smile.

One day, a teammate dragged me over to a game area we'd just set up. Together we raced around on tricycles, laughing and pedaling furiously.

It was a moment of pure fun that helped relieve the stress.

The final days of Jesus' life were more stressful than getting ready for that conference, and they are an important reminder for us.

Two days before the Passover, when Jesus was sharing in a meal with His disciples in Bethany, a woman came and anointed Him with an expensive jar of perfume.

Her action was joyful—perhaps even thoughtless—as she poured this extravagant luxury all over Jesus' head. Mark 14:3–7 tells us that many of the people watching were indignant and thought her actions wasteful. They chided her, saying she should have sold the perfume and used the money for charity.

Yet Jesus stood up for her, saying that she'd done something beautiful. He explained, "You always have the poor with you. . . . But you will not always have Me" (v. 7). He then told them about His impending death.

Jesus had a remarkable way of drawing people's attention back to what really matters: His presence.

We can have moments of joy, beauty, and wonder in the midst of our most stressful challenges because we are confident of His presence in His Word and in the sacraments of Baptism and the Lord's Supper that He gave us. Scripture assures us that Jesus is always with us. His sacrifice won the battle against death on our behalf. His will is always done. He will never leave us, no matter what we do or where we go. His grace and mercy will never run out.

As Romans 8:38–39 reminds us,

> For I am sure that neither death nor life, nor angels
> nor rulers, nor things present nor things to come,
> nor powers, nor height nor depth, nor anything

else in all creation, will be able to separate us
from the love of God in Christ Jesus our Lord.

These truths enable us to loosen our grip on the
steering wheel of our lives and enjoy the ride.

Questions

☐ Where are you experiencing the most stress this week?

☐ What's a moment of joy you've had, even in the middle
of your stress?

☐ Romans 8:38–39 tells us that nothing and no one can
separate us from the love of Christ. How does that
powerful truth comfort you?

....
....
....
....
....
....
....
....
....
....
....
....
....

1

John 20:26–27
SCARS TELL A STORY

O ne day when I was little, my bicycle broke and sent me careening down a steep hill. I face-planted in gravel, badly skinning my chin, knees, and hands.

The worst injury was my right palm. As I'd put my hands out in front of me, desperately trying to stop myself, a rock had sliced open my hand and lodged deep under my skin.

I was in agony: badly wounded, angry about my broken bike, and embarrassed that I'd fallen. My dad helped me home as I cried, holding my bloody hand and wincing in pain.

When I'm hurt, I usually get angry. And though I don't remember what I said, I'm sure I yelled at my dad on that long walk home. A lot.

I've been guilty of getting hurt—and angry—with God too. Have you?

Maybe you prayed for something, and it seems like God didn't answer your prayers. Or perhaps you find yourself in a hopeless situation and you're suffering when it's not even your fault. Possibly others have hurt you and let you down. Maybe it feels like God is just one more source of pain and frustration, and you're afraid to admit to yourself that you're angry with Him.

John 20 tells us about the account of Thomas, who refused to believe that Jesus was truly alive until he physically felt the holes in Jesus' hands where the soldiers had nailed Him to the cross. In the face of Thomas's doubt, Jesus responded by reaching out to him. As we read in John 20:26–27,

> Although the doors were locked, Jesus came and stood among them and said, "Peace be with you." Then He said to Thomas, "Put your finger here, and see My hands; and put out your hand, and place it in My side. Do not disbelieve, but believe."

Like Thomas, we sometimes push others away in our pain. We say we won't believe anything until we see it with our own eyes. We may even be guilty of pushing God away, angry and disappointed in our circumstances.

God never abandons us, however. God the Son came to Thomas with proof of His resurrection, and He comes to us in His Word, promising that the resurrection is ours too.

As my dad and I trudged home that day, nothing stopped him from patiently walking with me while I was angry and hurt. He took me into the kitchen, helped clean my wounds, and removed the rock from my hand. The blood, tears, and anger didn't scare him away from loving me and taking care of me. Even facing the worst of my temper and mess, my dad wasn't disgusted.

Neither is our heavenly Father.

Our scars tell a story. And part of that story is God's willingness to walk with us through every painful step, even when we're angry and shouting at Him or we run away from Him in anger.

That scar on my hand is a daily reminder of a terrible moment, but one in which I clearly received love and tender mercy.

Your scars can be a reminder that you receive God's tender compassion, no matter what hurt you endure.

Activity: Draw a comic strip of the worst injury you've ever dealt with. As you draw, how do you see that God cared for you in that difficult moment? How do Jesus' scars tell a story of God's love for you?

2

Psalm 73:26; 2 Corinthians 5:17–19
LIFE'S DETOURS

The moment stands out with absolute clarity.

It was chilly, and my soccer coach was yelling at us to pass the ball. I panted as I kicked hard, and I suddenly fell to my knees in agony.

It felt like someone had stabbed my leg. Tears streamed down my face as I rolled in pain. Unable to walk, I crawled off the field.

Over the course of many months and visits to multiple doctors, I was diagnosed with a micro-tear in my calf muscle.

Before this injury, I was a stellar athlete. I competed with the high school track team, even as a middle school student. But this injury, followed by months of physical therapy and pain, meant that my visions of athletic achievement disappeared. Overnight, the sports I loved so much—soccer, basketball, and track—became difficult for me to enjoy.

I felt lost. I didn't expect this massive disruption to my life. *This isn't fair*, I thought as I watched my teammates take my place while I sat on the sidelines.

You've probably encountered unexpected detours too. Maybe your parents divorced or you had to change schools or move to a new city. Perhaps death, a cancer diagnosis, or the betrayal of someone you care about jolted you onto a different path.

Sometimes these moments cause us to question God and ask why He's letting us deal with these problems. It can feel like life isn't fair. Or that God isn't paying attention to us. Or that we don't matter. Or that it'll never get better.

When our lives zig and zag in unexpected directions, we can hold on to one certainty: God is with us, no matter what. The Bible reminds us in Psalm 73:26,

> My flesh and my heart may fail, but God is the strength of my heart and my portion forever.

It turned out that my injury changed my life for the better. I was unable to compete at the same level, so I channeled my energy into writing, participating in various clubs, and meeting new friends. I pursued a degree in ministry, through which I've been blessed to publish books and speak all over the country.

> Therefore, if anyone is in Christ, he is a new creation. The old has passed away; behold, the new has come. All this is from God, who through Christ reconciled us to Himself and gave us the ministry of reconciliation; that is, in Christ God was reconciling the world to Himself, not counting their trespasses against them. (2 Corinthians 5:17–19)

I never would have expected my life to turn out the way it has, but that's the beauty of it—life is an adventure. You don't know what's around the corner, but there are always plenty of blessings to counteract any problems you encounter. You are part of the Body of Christ, so everything you do begins with following Jesus. You can be sure that whatever path you are on, the Holy Spirit works through you, strengthening your faith and developing your spiritual gifts so you can give glory to God and serve others.

Your life will be filled with unexpected detours and potholes too. But no matter where you go or what you face, God will be with you. He is the strength of your heart and your portion forever.

Faith Notes

....
....
....
....
....
....
....
....
....
....
....

3

1 Peter 5:7; Psalm 30:5

FINDING HOPE IN GRIEF

S everal years ago, I got an unexpected call from a parent while I was leading a mission trip for my middle school students.

His voice breaking with emotion, the father of one of my students informed me that his teenage niece had just been killed in a car accident. His son, her cousin, was on the mission trip with me, and his father wanted me to tell him. "They're so close," his dad cried, overcome with sorrow. "He's going to be devastated."

With a heavy heart, my leaders and I sat down to share the sad news with our student. As expected, he was gutted.

There's no easy way to tackle the subject of grief.

Saying goodbye to someone you love who is no longer living is one of the most awful, emotional, and stressful experiences you can ever have. Loss is a universal part of our lives, but just because we all go through it doesn't make it any easier.

I've lost friends and family, and I've cried alongside many young people who have lost friends and family of their own. The sorrow is real, and so are the feelings of regret and guilt, of confusion and anger. Grief is like pulling open a locker and letting everything inside just clatter out, one big jumbled mess.

Maybe you haven't yet experienced that kind of grief. Unfortunately, because we live in a broken world, you will. But Christians can face it with a sense of peace because we know that the Holy Spirit is at work in our lives to strengthen our faith in Jesus and that, someday, we will rejoice in heaven and be free of all pain and sadness.

If you're struggling with grief, acknowledge your pain and bring it to God. After all, He knows what it means to navigate sorrow. Remember the account in John 11 of Jesus grieving the death of His friend Lazarus? Even though Jesus knew He would raise Lazarus from the dead, He still wept. His tears are evidence of His compassion for His people and of the pain that earthly death brings.

In times of loss, seek comfort in Christ. As 1 Peter 5:7 reminds us, we can share our troubles with Jesus,

Casting all your anxieties on Him, because He cares for you.

Our grief won't last forever, as Psalm 30:5 comforts us with the truth that

Weeping may tarry for the night, but
joy comes with the morning.

We find hope in grief because we have a God who serves as our refuge in the midst of the darkness. Scripture tells us again and again that God is close to those who mourn. He understands our overwhelming emotions and offers us His comfort as a healing balm.

Grief is a journey that God walks with us, lending us His strength and surrounding us with people who remind us of His love.

Faith Notes

....
....
....
....
....
....
....
....
....
....
....
....
....
....
....
....
....
....
....
....

4

Colossians 3:23–24
RESPONSIBILITY

I 'll be back in a bit!" I yelled out the window as I dropped my youth off at the health center where they were showering while on a mission trip to Chattanooga.

As I pulled up to the curb, they shoved backpacks and snacks all over the back seat in their haste to hit the locker rooms. The van full of students quickly emptied. As I slowly drove the van away from the curb and turned the corner toward a gas station down the street, I heard a loud *whoosh.*

I looked in the rearview mirror but didn't see anything. *It must have been a backpack falling,* I thought.

Then I heard sloshing.

As quickly as I could, I pulled over. When I opened the sliding doors to the van, a waterfall of Gatorade cascaded over my feet. Apparently, someone had balanced a full five-gallon cooler of Gatorade on the edge of the seat while leaving the van. It had tipped over and spilled everywhere.

When I walked into the gas station to pay, my shoes squeaking on the linoleum, the cashier grinned at me. "I saw the whole thing," he laughed, taking my card.

"I don't know what you do for a living, but whatever it is, they need to pay you more."

Despite me grilling the students when I got back, nobody confessed to his or her irresponsible behavior with the cooler. It had taken me quite a bit of time to clean the van, and my shoes were ruined. As funny as the story is now, I was peeved at the time about bearing the burden of someone else's bad choice.

Responsibility is a mindset, not a singular action. Irresponsible choices that we may think aren't a big deal, like littering or speeding, may cause more damage than we realize.

God gave Adam and Eve the responsibility of caring for His creation, and that privilege has been passed down to us. To be good stewards of the blessings that God has given us, we should treat ourselves and the rest of creation—people, places, plants, and animals—with value.

Colossians 3:23–24 stresses the importance of knowing that what we do on earth matters:

Whatever you do, work heartily, as for the Lord and not for men, knowing that from the Lord you will receive the inheritance as your reward. You are serving the Lord Christ.

Being responsible means you think before you act and you follow through when you make a promise. It means you treat possessions and property with care. It involves respecting your own body, mind, and soul, and extending that respect to others' bodies, minds, and souls. Responsible people also admit to the times when they've made a mistake—maybe they've forgotten something, hurt someone, or broken an item.

Or maybe they even balanced a cooler on the edge of a van seat.

Embracing responsibility shows that you value yourself and others. It honors God's creation and creates harmony, which is sorely needed in our world today.

When we see mess in the world around us, when we deal with someone else's careless actions, we can remember that Jesus bears the burden of our sin and mistakes and thoughtlessness. He cleans up the mess we leave behind and pays for it fully.

As you serve Jesus by your daily actions, live in the grace He freely offers.

Activity

In what area do you need to embrace a little more responsibility?

Circle one: people, places, plants, animals

What's one way you can show that you value God's creation?

....
....
....
....
....
....

5

Proverbs 27:17
LOSING FRIENDS

I stepped into the coffee shop, breathing in the familiar scent. It had been years since I'd been here, but it felt like I was right back in those days when the memories were made, lounging on the couch with my best friends. We'd spent so many hours in this coffee shop.

The trip down memory lane was colored with sadness. Those friends and I had parted ways years ago, as our lives headed in different directions. Although I'd tried to stay in touch with some of them, distance and time had ended our friendship.

Friendships change for a lot of reasons. You may drift apart over a long period of time or suddenly experience a blow out that severs connection. When experiencing this, it's normal to struggle with grief. Maybe you've lost that one person you vented to the most or the person you thought you could trust with your secrets.

Sometimes you lose an entire group of friends. The fallout changes everything—where you sit at lunch, what teams and clubs you want to be on, and what your after-school routine looks like.

Losing friends can be depressing, confusing, and painful. It can affect your outlook on life and your feelings about yourself. You may experience emotions of hopelessness and anger when friends disappear from your life.

Here's the truth, though: even though friendships change, God does not change. His love for you never ends. He never abandons you, ignores you, or rejects you.

The loss of a friendship creates a hole that only God can help heal. Trust that He will bring precious relationships into your life to support and encourage you. Be open to connecting with new friends, even though you have been hurt. As Proverbs 27:17 reminds us,

Iron sharpens iron, and one man sharpens another.

God designed us to be in community with one another. And although life in this sinful world means we encounter fractured friendships, we can be confident that God will bring good people into our lives to bring out the best in us.

Even when you can't see it, be confident that God is creating a wonderful future for you, according to His will, and He will be with you as you embark on it. No matter what, His love for you will never run out or change. God looks at you through the work of His Son, Jesus, who stands before God as your Advocate, Intercessor, and Savior.

He alone is your best friend for life. Journal about what a difference that knowledge makes in your life.

6

Proverbs 14:1
DON'T RUIN IT

H ave you ever watched a video online where people create obstacle courses in their yards for wildlife? The most common ones I've seen have been creative homeowners who make zany contraptions for squirrels. In video after video, I've seen poor squirrels try to scale difficult feeders, wind through tiny mazes, and be launched from spinning platforms—all in pursuit of a walnut.

While it may be amusing to watch someone thwart a small animal, these actions parallel some self-sabotaging behaviors that we sometimes employ in our own lives. Often, we engage in these actions without knowing what we're doing or why, but the consequences are nevertheless troubling. Instead of experiencing community, as God intended, we isolate ourselves and maybe even wreck relationships.

What does it look like to ruin a relationship, intentionally or unintentionally?

It can be the act of pushing people away as they start to get close to you. You might find yourself ghosting others or ignoring overtures of a friend who is trying to fix what has been broken. Alternately, you might lash out angrily at someone, giving them a reason to back off. Maybe you gossip and badmouth without caring, allowing it to rupture relationships. Or perhaps you try to control someone, making unrealistic demands on their time and attention then walking away from the relationship when they fail to live up to your expectations.

Proverbs 14:1 tells us,

> The wisest of women builds her house, but folly with her own hands tears it down.

In your life, are you building up or tearing apart the connections you have with others?

The act of sabotaging relationships stems from insecurity and unhealthy coping mechanisms within us. Sometimes it comes from difficult experiences in your childhood. Other times, we emulate poor behavior that has been modeled to us by our family or friends. But however we learned to act this way, it's important to recognize that it is not productive and will only cause harm.

God gives us a plan for treating others well. You might remember it as the second table of the Law—Commandments Four through Ten. Living in community with others involves showing forgiveness and letting kind, encouraging words come out of our mouths. Scripture gives us plenty of advice on letting go of resentment and choosing reconciliation, growth, and healing throughout our lives. Over all of this is the transformative power of grace, given freely to us through Jesus' sacrifice on the cross.

It's up to you to honestly reckon with your negative behaviors and resolve to be different—to repent. Just because you grew up learning something does not mean it needs to be a mistake you continue throughout your life. Your future can be about building bridges, not barriers.

With God's help, by the power of the Holy Spirit, you can work through unhealthy patterns and emerge stronger and healthier, wrapped in the grace that Jesus gives so abundantly.

Faith Notes

....
....
....
....
....
....
....
....
....
....
....
....
....
....
....
....

7

Ephesians 4:29
REAL UGLINESS

I sat in the lobby of the hotel with an acquaintance at a conference we were attending. Together, we smiled and waved at a colleague before my acquaintance settled into her seat. "Guess what I heard about him," she whispered.

Although I listened to her commentary, I realized in real time that she was displaying some ugly behavior. I also realized that by continuing the conversation, I was complicit in it. As soon as I could, I excused myself and left. You see, you never look good when you're trying to make somebody else look bad.

We like to think our words are harmless, but our tongues carry immense power. The comments we make can destroy someone's reputation or self-esteem. And we know this. We may try to defend ourselves by saying that we're just venting or that we didn't really mean it, but the reality is that this is ugly behavior. Reality shows, videos, and memes show us all sorts of catty, negative behavior that people engage in.

Whether it is hurtful, mocking words or jealous gossip, the impact of this behavior is damaging and it's contrary to how God wants us to live. Ephesians 4:29 tells us,

Let no corrupting talk come out of your mouths, but only such as is good for building up, as fits the occasion, that it may give grace to those who hear.

Each of us has the choice to use kind, encouraging words or to use ugly ones. We can choose to build or destroy. Our actions stem from the condition of our hearts, which should be full of gratitude for the love Jesus showed us by taking on the pain and punishment our sin caused.

If you're struggling with ugliness, take time to admit that you're a sinful person who strays into gossip, and repent by not going there again. Yes, I know this is difficult. It's much easier to join in the gossip. So ask God to help you overcome this. And be assured that despite your shortcomings, God still calls you His beloved, forgiven child. He meets your mistakes with grace. And you can extend His grace to others and grow in maturity in handling relationships. When you do, you honor God and help spread beauty—not ugliness—in the world.

Activity

Think about how often you engage in ugly behavior. Do you frequently gossip? make fun of others? damage other people's reputation or self-esteem? use your words to tear down instead of build up? Spend some time praying about how to live in God's love and share it with others. What is one behavior you might change and one new behavior you might embrace?

1

Matthew 18:21–22

FORGIVING . . . EVEN WHEN YOU DON'T FEEL LIKE IT

I stood on the cold sand, listening to the waves crash in front of us, and watched tears stream down the face of the student standing with me. Our youth group was on a weekend trip to the beach, and one of the students had come down to the shore with me after our evening devotion to share some personal struggles.

My student sobbed as she told me about hurtful words from her stepmom and her despair over the fractured relationship she had with her dad. Despite laughing with her friends all day, her sadness lurked under the surface, emotional wounds raw and festering.

When others hurt us, our emotions can feel like a wave threatening to sweep us away. Whether it's a close friend, family member, classmate, teacher, or coach who lets us down, the pain can seem unbearable.

The more you value the relationship, the more it hurts when it crumbles.

Jesus knew all about this despair. In the New Testament, we read about how He was betrayed by one of His disciples, Judas, and handed over to be crucified.

Yet Jesus endured the pain, knowing that saving us from our sin was worth the immense cost.

Perhaps you've heard the phrase "Unforgiveness is like drinking poison and hoping the other person dies." While you may not literally have that murderous vibe, you're probably guilty of wishing pain on a person who has hurt you.

You might be tempted to gossip about a friend who has betrayed you or badmouth a teacher who made a comment you didn't like. Perhaps your instincts are even darker, and you want to make someone suffer like you have.

The Bible points us away from revenge, however, and straight into the arms of Jesus. He understands the hurt, and He alone can provide comfort that soothes your soul.

In Matthew 18:21–22, Peter asked Jesus how many times he should forgive those who hurt him:

> Then Peter came up and said to Him, "Lord, how often will my brother sin against me, and I forgive him? As many as seven times?" Jesus said to him, "I do not say to you seven times, but seventy-seven times."

Choosing to forgive won't automatically make things easier or better, but it will be an act of obedience to living the way God wants you to live. We trust Him when He instructs us, knowing that His ways are better than ours.

Even when we don't always feel like forgiving, we trust in the One who freely extends forgiveness to us. Journal about how His forgiveness makes you feel.

2

2 Timothy 1:7; Romans 3:23–24
WHEN YOU'VE BECOME SOMEONE YOU HATE

One of the major turning points in my life came when I made a bully cry.

I know. You don't know whether to like me more or less when you hear that.

My classmates had been tortured by a mean student for years. Early on, I stood up to this bully by defending the shy kids in my class. I saw myself as a protector, someone who was doing good.

In time, however, my actions crossed the line into bullying this student back. One day, I took it too far. I secretly convinced my entire class to join in hurting the feelings of our bully.

As I sat behind this bully after everyone had been mean to her, watching her shoulders heave with silent tears, I was suddenly ashamed. I'd strayed so far from the kind person I wanted to be—I'd deeply hurt someone. Even though she'd been teasing my classmates for a long time, I couldn't bring myself to continue to get even. Revenge wasn't worth it. Neither was the shame my own behavior caused.

In that moment, I promised myself I would treat others better. I recognized that I had leadership abilities, but I was using them selfishly instead of blessing others with the gifts God had given me. I clung to the truth I found in 2 Timothy 1:7:

> For God gave us a spirit not of fear but of
> power and love and of self-control.

Years later, this bully tracked me down online. As we connected on social media, I discovered that she'd had a hard life. At rock bottom, though, she'd become a Christian and turned her behavior around. She's now healthy, happy, and a sister in Christ.

I was guilty of hurting someone, just like my class bully was guilty of hurting others. We're all sinful people in need of saving, as Romans 3:23–24 tells us:

> For all have sinned and fall short of the glory
> of God, and are justified by His grace as a gift,
> through the redemption that is in Christ Jesus.

We are justified—made right—in Christ. His sacrifice negates all the terrible things we do to others. And although we will likely deal with the earthly consequences of our mistakes in this life, we can be confident that our eternity is sealed with a Savior who loves us. And that knowledge allows us to confess, repent, and start over.

Whether we bully or have been bullied, use our God-given gifts properly or abuse them, hurt or love the people around us, we know that Jesus welcomes us into His arms with understanding, compassion, and forgiveness.

We are not defined by what we do or what's been done to us. Our identity comes from being the baptized, beloved children of God.

Activity

Reflect on someone you've hurt, consciously or unconsciously. What happened? When? What role did your words or actions play? Write that person's name on the lines below and fill in a short prayer of repentance for the damage you've done to that person. After writing your prayer, consider if the Holy Spirit is prompting you to reach out and ask for forgiveness. If so, prayerfully reflect on how you might reach out to restore this relationship.

....
....
....
....
....
....
....
....
....
....
....
....
....

3

Ephesians 4:26
ANGER OVERLOAD

Read this list and check any of the things that make you irrationally angry:

- ☐ slow walkers

- ☐ stepping on something wet when you're wearing socks

- ☐ when the internet connection just drops

- ☐ stubbing your toe

- ☐ people who cut in line

- ☐ people who try to talk to you when you're on the phone with someone else

- ☐ having someone read over your shoulder

- ☐ people who tell you to calm down or cheer up when you're not angry or upset

- ☐ when you pour a bowl of cereal and then find out there's no milk left

- ☐ pop-up ads

- ☐ people who push the elevator button after you just pushed it

- ☐ when you charge your phone and come back an hour later to find out you didn't plug in the charger

- ☐ people who stop in the middle of the walkway and force you to walk around them

- ☐ loaning money to a friend who will never pay you back

- ☐ when someone turns on the lights when you're obviously sleeping

- ☐ people who chew with their mouths open

- ☐ trying to find the end of a roll of tape

Anger is a part of our daily lives. While it's normal to feel angry sometimes, and anger is one of the emotions God created us to have, He wants us to handle it in an appropriate way. Ephesians 4:26 tells us,

> Be angry and do not sin; do not let the
> sun go down on your anger.

While anger itself isn't necessarily a sin, the way we respond to it can be. If we cling to anger and let it fester, making us bitter and resentful, this can lead to sin. God encourages us to deal with our anger immediately, seeking resolution and reconciliation as quickly as we can.

Spend time in prayer, asking the Holy Spirit to give you the wisdom to work through your rage and use it to refine rather than engulf you. And in those moments when you lose your cool completely, go to Jesus, confess the sinful thoughts and ways of your emotions, resolve to change your behaviors, and receive His forgiveness.

4

Proverbs 28:13

ADMITTING YOU'RE WRONG

Have you ever heard the adage "It's not about how many times you fall down; it's about how many times you get back up"?

I sure relate to that. My life is a testament to many times when I've fallen down, made mistakes, hurt others, and let people down. Your life is likely full of your own list of struggles, failures, and disappointments.

In life, we're bound to fall down from time to time. None of us is perfect, which means none of us can avoid making the occasional wrong turn or stumbling into a pothole. It's not so much about avoiding those roadblocks, though, as it is about how we deal with them. As Christians, we can admit that we're sinful people navigating through a broken world and that we need a Savior to embrace us and lift us back on our feet when we inevitably fall.

Yet, admitting when we're wrong isn't easy, even when we know that God's grace covers over our mistakes. We worry about what people will think or how our parents will react or what the consequences will be. Our world tempts us to hide our flaws and failures, pretending we're fine.

Proverbs 28:13 tells us,

Whoever conceals his transgressions will not prosper, but he who confesses and forsakes them will obtain mercy.

When we are open about admitting our mistakes, we find a merciful God waiting for us with open arms. He doesn't hold our failures against us but wipes the slate clean, forgiving us each time we fall down. His love for us doesn't change, and that helps remind us that true acceptance is found in our identity as children of God, not in the opinions of others.

The next time you fall down, don't beat yourself up or try to hide it. Instead, confess your mistakes to God and to those who need to know them. Ask for forgiveness. Resolve to stop the negative behavior. And trust that in Jesus, God loves you unconditionally no matter what you've done.

When we admit when we're wrong, it can serve as a powerful beacon to others about how God's grace shines in our weakest moments. Your story is your own, full of triumphs and failures—just like everyone else's story is also full of triumphs and failures.

Have the courage to be real about your struggles and about the mercies that God gives you every day.

Faith Notes

....

....

1
John 3:16–17
BEING BOLD

W hat would you do for $100? Would you sing a song out loud in front of your classmates? Would you wear a hideous outfit in public or eat something gross?

When something is important to us, we are emboldened to take action. Sometimes the attainment of what is important to us means pushing past what we're comfortable with saying or doing. It may mean acting out of character or taking a risk, even if you're not sure what the outcome may be.

Nicodemus was a man who demonstrated boldness in pursuit of what was important: getting to know Jesus. In John 3, we see the account of Nicodemus, a Pharisee and member of the Sanhedrin (the Jewish governing council), approaching Jesus with deep questions. Nicodemus was an important man, one who others looked to for answers. He risked his position and his reputation to talk to Jesus, which shows us just how important he knew Jesus to be.

It was during this conversation with Nicodemus that Jesus uttered what may be the best-known words from the entire Bible. John 3:16–17 captures an incredible truth that came from their encounter:

For God so loved the world, that He gave His only Son, that whoever believes in Him should not perish but have eternal life. For God did not send His Son into the world to condemn the world, but in order that the world might be saved through Him.

Jesus met Nicodemus's curiosity with grace and acceptance. Nicodemus's questions didn't scare Jesus or make Him angry or frustrated. Instead, Jesus spent time explaining important spiritual truths about repentance, spiritual rebirth, and salvation.

This bold action that Nicodemus took risked his reputation but it resulted in the best possible gift: the gift of learning about Jesus' unconditional love.

Through his conversation with Jesus, Nicodemus learned that faith is a gift from God. It's not something we can create or earn for ourselves but something we receive through the work of the Holy Spirit at our Baptism and that is strengthened when we receive Holy Communion. The Holy Spirit within us leads us to embrace the saving grace of Jesus. Some people choose to reject God's free gift of salvation, but He continues to extend it to us no matter how far we've drifted away from Him.

Be bold in the pursuit of a genuine relationship with Jesus, your Savior. Like Nicodemus, don't let your reputation, messy past, or current situation prevent you from learning more about the God who loves you fiercely.

God is ready to meet all your questions with grace and acceptance too. Journal questions you might ask Him.

2

Matthew 6:14–15

GIVING SOMEONE A SECOND CHANCE

A routine conversation about small group Bible study somehow turned into a hurtful conversation in which a mom insulted me and screamed at me. I had no idea what I'd done wrong, but I was humiliated and angry about the way I'd been treated.

Upset, I sought counsel from a coworker. "It's probably not about you as much as it is something else," he told me. "I'd bet she's dealing with something and just took her anger out on you because you were the closest target."

"Well, I'm not going to talk to her ever again," I huffed, still hurt.

"That's not how God wants you to handle it," my coworker replied. "Take some time to pray about this and calm down, then meet with her and work it out."

As angry as I was, I knew he was right. After a few days of prayerful contemplation, I was still pretty mad, but I knew that forgiveness was the choice I had to make, whether or not this mom acknowledged her wrongdoing.

I sat down with the mom, who confessed that her own mother had just been diagnosed with terminal cancer. "I was upset about that and didn't process it well. I wasn't actually angry with you. Will you forgive me?"

We're all sinful people who mess up. Sometimes our mistakes are compounded by difficult circumstances and other times they're a byproduct of our selfishness.

But just as God doesn't hold our mistakes against us, we shouldn't hold mistakes against others. Forgiveness is hard, but it's a decision we make despite the emotions we feel. While forgiving doesn't mean you forget, it does mean that you choose to move past being hurt and focus on embracing healing. Holding a grudge only causes resentment and anger to fester within you. Don't be surprised if deep wounds take a lot of time—and multiple decisions—to forgive. In Matthew 6:14–15, Jesus tells us,

> For if you forgive others their trespasses, your heavenly Father will also forgive you, but if you do not forgive others their trespasses, neither will your Father forgive your trespasses.

Jesus freely offers us forgiveness, and it doesn't hinge on our ability to admit all our shortcomings. He knows we are sinful by nature, and He still chose to trade His life for us to be saved. His desire is for us to extend that same grace to others in order to point everyone toward the eternal life found in Christ alone.

The next time you find yourself wounded, choose to forgive. Let each decision to forgive be a reminder of the forgiveness that Jesus has given to you.

3

Romans 8:26–27
UNCONDITIONAL LOVE

Every single time I open the door, he's there for me. He never judges my sighs. Never asks annoying questions when I'm in a bad mood. No matter how irritated I am, he always greets me with pure, sweet joy. Even if I yell at him, he just moves in closer to comfort me. He never holds a grudge and never hurts my feelings.

Yes, I'm clearly talking about my dog.

We all want to be loved just as we are; to be known completely, on a deep level; and to live connected to others. But outside of your dog, it's difficult to find unconditional acceptance.

This desire to be known inside and out and loved despite all our flaws is a powerful urge. Despite our attempts to find this sort of deep, lasting love in relationships or by throwing ourselves into school or work or hobbies, we cannot find this level of acceptance outside of Jesus.

The Bible reminds us that God knows us so well that He can interpret even the groans we utter when we can't come up with words to express our emotions. As Romans 8:26–27 says,

> Likewise the Spirit helps us in our weakness. For we do not know what to pray for as we ought, but the Spirit Himself intercedes for us with groanings too deep for words. And He who searches our hearts knows what is the mind of the Spirit, because the Spirit intercedes for the saints according to the will of God.

What a comfort to know that even when we can't articulate our feelings, God knows and empathizes with us. No matter what emotions grip us or what we encounter in life, God's love is constant. Nothing can separate us from the love of Christ, our Savior.

Jesus' unconditional love, acceptance of our flaws, and boundless mercy give us a peace that no one or nothing else can offer.

Not even your sweet puppy can hold a candle to the love that Christ lavishes on you.

Faith Notes

....
....
....
....
....
....
....
....

4

Matthew 5:16

EVERYDAY MISSIONARIES

Have you ever been on a mission trip? In my years as a youth leader, I've taken hundreds of students on mission trips to many places.

The mission trip that impacted me most was when I went to a poor city in Cuba several years ago. Although the people we shared Jesus with were impoverished, they shared everything they had with us. I vividly remember visiting a tiny one-room house, the dirt floor dry and dusty underfoot, and squatting down to talk to a little boy.

We asked to see his toys, and he grinned and picked up a faded Mickey Mouse stuffed animal. Looking around, I realized that this child possessed only that one solitary toy. Nevertheless, he held it out to me to play with.

If you ever get the chance to go on a mission trip, I highly recommend it. It changes you for the better and impacts those you serve in remarkable ways.

People typically sign up for mission trips so they can have a meaningful experience sharing their faith. But the reality is that our mission isn't lived out on trips alone. God intends for us to live lives of meaning, serving as everyday missionaries to the world around us. Matthew 5:16 reminds us,

> In the same way, let your light shine before others, so that they may see your good works and give glory to your Father who is in heaven.

As Christians, we have the opportunity to live in a manner that reflects the love and goodness of Jesus in our everyday lives. Through our words and actions, we can point others to Him. Being a missionary to your own circle of friends and family may change the future of the people around you for eternity.

What does your mission field look like? Is it the soccer team, the gaming community, or your friends who love anime? Has God positioned you to share the Good News with your coworkers at the grocery store or the kids who sit at the cool table?

As much as they may hide it, everyone you know is broken, struggling, and in need of a Savior. Perhaps the Holy Spirit's plan is to use you to connect someone to Jesus.

Ask God to give you eyes to see those who need to hear about Him, a mouth to share His truth and love, and feet that are willing to go wherever He leads in order to reach those who need to know the Lord and the promise of salvation.

Faith Notes

5

John 16:33

SAILING THROUGH OUR TRIALS

One of the perks of going to college in Southern California was getting to spend time soaking up the sun at the beach, by the pool, and on my friends' kayaks.

Over spring break one year, a few of my friends and I camped at Huntington Beach. It was a wonderful week together, and it culminated in our friend's dad taking us all sailing one afternoon.

Contrary to what I'd imagined, sailing was a ton of work. Sure, there were moments of sheer bliss as we coasted effortlessly through the turquoise water and felt the wind whip across our faces. But more often, sailing involved a lot of effort. Our captain was constantly adjusting ropes and sails. His work revolved around careful maneuvers, perseverance, and sheer grit. Sometimes we slowed to a standstill, and it took time to find the wind and move again.

Sailing is a lot like life. It's moments of staggering wonder and joy coupled with determination and resiliency. Life is filled with challenges and moments when it feels like we've hit a standstill and we're stuck.

In these moments, it's critical that we turn to the One who guides our lives.

Jesus reminds us that this temporary life on earth is going to be full of struggles—it won't always be smooth sailing. As He says in John 16:33,

> I have said these things to you, that in Me you may have peace. In the world you will have tribulation. But take heart; I have overcome the world.

While challenges will always be a part of our lives, we can find solace in Jesus, who already conquered sin, death, and the devil for us.

Life's trials are opportunities for us to grow and deepen our relationship with Christ. Even when times are tough and it feels like you're not going anywhere, trust that God's got you.

The next time you're sailing along and suddenly drift to a halt, remember that God is in control. He is faithful and will steer you through every challenge.

Faith Notes

....
....
....
....
....
....
....

6

Jeremiah 1:6–8; 1 Timothy 4:12
TOO YOUNG

. . . .

K ari and I sat up late one night during our first year of college, talking about our imagined futures. We were friends in the same undergrad program, studying to be directors of Christian education.

Kari had grown up with a youth leader she adored and absorbed a lot of wisdom from, but I had never even been in youth group. In fact, I was the only one in my whole college class who hadn't regularly attended a small group or gone to Christian summer camp. What came easily to everyone else because of their experience was brand new to me.

I confided to Kari that I was nervous about someday being a youth leader. "I don't know if God can use me," I expressed.

Kari smiled and shared a quote with me that I still think about all the time: "God doesn't call the qualified; He qualifies the called."

Have you ever worried that God can't use you because you're too inexperienced, uneducated, shy, or young?

The account of Jeremiah in the Old Testament is one worth knowing. He was just a young man when

God called him to return to his homeland, Israel, and convince his people to repent and turn back to God. It was a serious mission, and Jeremiah expressed his doubts to God, saying, "I do not know how to speak, for I am only a youth" (Jeremiah 1:6).

God's response to Jeremiah was one of calm reassurance that He is in control:

> But the LORD said to me, "Do not say, 'I am only a youth'; for to all to whom I send you, you shall go, and whatever I command you, you shall speak. Do not be afraid of them, for I am with you to deliver you, declares the LORD." (Jeremiah 1:7–8)

God doesn't examine our qualifications before calling us to share His message of grace with the world. He fully knows our age, weaknesses, and shortcomings and still promises to give us His strength. As 1 Timothy 4:12 reminds us,

> Let no one despise you for your youth, but set the believers an example in speech, in conduct, in love, in faith, in purity.

In those moments where you feel too young, too bashful, or too inexperienced, trust that our almighty God is with you and will protect you. Through the Holy Spirit, He will give you the words to speak and guide you to the people He wants you to encounter. Trust that sharing the Gospel of Jesus isn't dependent on you—it happens because God is working through you.

You're never not enough to embrace God's calling.

7

Psalm 18:2

HEALING FROM HURT INFLICTED BY OTHERS

I had barely gotten off the phone with one sobbing college student before I received a frantic text.

"Help me," it said, panic evident in the words. "Something happened to me and I don't know what to do."

These two young women, both lovely Christian girls, had encountered violent behavior from aggressive men. Although these two girls didn't even know each other and their assaults hadn't happened on exactly the same day, they were both coming to me for counsel and comfort at nearly the same time.

It was an intensely emotional, difficult situation for me, and I wasn't even the one who'd been traumatized.

As beautiful as life is, it also contains moments of pain. Others can inflict serious physical, mental, or emotional pain on us. They can rob us of our innocence, destroy our self-confidence, and tempt us to feel like life isn't worth living.

While this may not be your reality, it's certainly the hell that many young people find themselves living. Statistically, one in four women will deal with abuse or aggression in her lifetime. In other words, if it hasn't happened to you, then it has happened to a friend, classmate, teacher, or even a parent.

Those whose lives are touched by violence and abuse often feel helpless and alone, unsure of what to share and who to talk to. Perhaps you don't want to get someone in trouble or deal with the shame of sharing the truth aloud. Your fears may lock you into a pattern of isolation, and keeping secrets like this prevents you from healing and moving on from what happened to you.

The Bible assures us that even in the worst moments we face, God is our refuge. He is there for us, no matter what we've done or had done to us. Psalm 18:2 says,

> The LORD is my rock and my fortress and my deliverer,
> my God, my rock, in whom I take refuge, my shield,
> and the horn of my salvation, my stronghold.

If you or someone you know has experienced abuse, assault, or any form of mistreatment, you are not alone. Don't suffer in isolation, hiding your pain from others. No matter what mistakes you may have made, you didn't ask for someone to hurt you the way they did.

Trust that God has compassion for you and has surrounded you with people who desire for you to feel safe and start the healing process. Reach out to trusted family, friends, and professionals who can support you. Call a hotline, or talk to the police or a trusted adult about what you're going through.

Don't give up, because God will never give up on you.

As hopeless as we often feel, our God is mightier than anything or anyone. He promises to make a way when it seems impossible. He extends grace and forgiveness when we cling to shame. He provides hope and comfort when the darkness threatens to overwhelm—remember that Jesus has overcome the darkness of evil.

You are safe in the hands of our mighty Healer, and He alone can help you overcome the pain inflicted by others. You are not alone in any struggle you face, and Jesus is preparing a hope-filled future for you even now.

Faith Notes

....
....
....
....
....
....
....
....
....
....
....
....
....
....
....

8

Galatians 5:1
UNHEALTHY CONTROL

A young woman recently told me about her breakup with her boyfriend.

"I didn't even realize how controlling he was until I tried to end it with him," she recalled. "He'd isolated me from all my friends and family and always pointed out everyone's faults, especially mine. I had to check in with him all the time, even if I was just going to class. I was miserable and didn't even realize how awful I felt."

This story is all too common. Whether it's a boyfriend or close friend who's too controlling, the reality is that many of us find ourselves trapped in unhealthy relationships. This is not God's design for friendships or dating relationships, and it's definitely not good for your mental health.

In Galatians 5:1, we read,

> For freedom Christ has set us free; stand firm therefore, and do not submit again to a yoke of slavery.

Christ set us free from the chains of sin. In Him, we find the epitome of perfect love and compassion. To enjoy the freedom that Jesus offers, we cannot be trapped in unhealthy relationships, especially if they interfere with our faith, health, and well-being.

As you're still learning to navigate relationships, it can be challenging to ascertain when someone is being too controlling. Often, controlling behavior looks like interest and affection at first but snowballs the longer you're in a relationship, including friendship, so it can be difficult to identify. Small attempts at manipulation and disrespect can grow more frequent and serious as time goes on. Unfortunately, it can be hard to distance yourself when you're emotionally close to someone who's being too controlling.

The red flags of an overly controlling relationship can include the following:

☐ Manipulation and Control: If someone tries to control your decisions, actions, and opinions or manipulates your feelings, these are indications of an unhealthy relationship.

☐ Isolating Behavior: If someone tries to cut you off from your family or friends, your coach or counselor, or anyone else in your life, that's a problem. Often, a controlling person wants to make him- or herself the center of your life and demands your full attention. Healthy people are happy to see the person they love supported by a community.

☐ Abusive Attitude: If someone is showing signs of verbal, emotional, or physical abuse—including insulting words, threatening language, or pushing you around—this behavior is entirely inappropriate. A person who hurts others is not honoring God and needs accountability for his or her actions.

☐ Ignoring Boundaries: In healthy relationships, people respect each other and their preferences. If someone ignores your beliefs, feelings, or boundaries, or pushes you to do things you don't want to do, that's a problem.

If you worry that you or a friend may be stuck in an unhealthy relationship, talk about your concerns with a trusted adult, ministry professional, or counselor. Listen to that person's perspective and allow him or her to help you make decisions. Such a person wants you or your friend to be safe, after all.

What a blessing to know that God desires for His children to be happy and supported. His desire is for you to see a glimpse of His unconditional love through His people. Don't be afraid to detach from unhealthy relationships in your quest to honor God with your life. Trust that no matter what you go through, He is with you.

Faith Notes

....

....

....

....

....

....

....

9

Ephesians 5:2
HOW TO TREAT GUYS

You know how you're confused, feeling pressure, and trying to figure out this whole life thing?

Teenage guys are right there with you too.

The world gives us many mixed messages about men and women. It is the topic of thousands of books, millions of movies and songs and videos, and countless conversations. It's important for men and women to be in each other's lives in healthy, appropriate ways, as God intended for us to exist in community with one another.

I've worked with thousands of teenage boys in my career and had the chance to interview several for this devotion. In no uncertain terms, they told me how important it is for girls to treat guys with respect, extending Christ's love to them.

Ephesians 5:2 extols us to

Walk in love, as Christ loved us and gave Himself up for us.

Jesus demonstrated this sacrificial love as He gave Himself for us on the cross, and it guides us as we interact with others, including guys.

Even though they may seem tough, guys need empathy and compassion too.

Everyone you know is trying to figure out life. Offer your support and encouragement to men, helping to create a safe way for guys to feel valued. By asking the young men around you about their day or how they're handling things, you can extend friendship.

"If a guy shows his emotions, the last thing a girl should do is take them for granted," Robby wisely told me. A college student just starting his career playing Division I football, Robby has deep faith in Jesus and strives to glorify Him even in a culture that doesn't traditionally encourage guys to be vulnerable.

"Many men are scared to open up to people, so when it does happen, you should treat their emotions with respect," Robby shared. "I don't know that some women fully comprehend the level of trust it takes for a man to open up about his feelings with a woman."

Communicate openly with guys, paying attention to their perspectives but honestly sharing your own thoughts and opinions. Men and women need each other and add great value to each other's lives, but one gender isn't better or more talented than another. Avoid putting down, teasing, or dismissing men. Rather, model how Jesus interacted with people and let your words be those of wisdom, love, and truth. Don't toy with guys or play games, despite what you may see others do. Your brothers in Christ deserve honest words and respectful behavior.

Be patient with the guys in your life, knowing that growth takes time and that young women tend to be further along in emotional development than young men. Don't try to change men, but respect who God has made them to be and inspire them with your own growth. Pray for them and look for ways to share what your faith means to you. Maintain your personal boundaries but do so with understanding and grace.

When you walk in the way of Jesus' love as you deal with guys, you'll be honoring Him and contributing to the building of positive, God-honoring relationships.

Faith Notes

....
....
....
....
....
....
....
....
....
....
....
....
....
....

10

Matthew 5:9
BE A PEACEMAKER

There's always one person who stirs up dissension. You know the one I'm talking about: The first one to forward the snarky text. The one with screenshots of all the private conversations. The one who makes the face behind others' backs. The one who whispers and mocks and plays people against each other.

Maybe this person is you (if you're being honest).

When people behave in a toxic manner, their words and actions negatively impact everyone around them. This isn't how God intends for us to live. In a world marred by conflict, we are called to be peacemakers. As Matthew 5:9 reminds us,

> Blessed are the peacemakers, for they shall be called sons of God.

Peace in our world means unity, the intersection of understanding and reconciliation. While you may not be serving as an ambassador navigating a treaty between warring countries, you reflect Jesus and the love and grace He extends to you as He reconciles you to your heavenly Father.

This means you have the ability to build bridges and resolve squabbles among your friends, siblings, and family members. The impact of your actions may affect your school, workplace, and home. When we embrace our role as peacemakers, as God's children, we become change agents.

So, what behavior does a peacemaker model?

- ☐ Peacemakers forgive, extending God's grace to those who have wronged them. They refuse to live in anger or hold on to grudges; rather, they seek to live in harmony with others.

- ☐ Peacemakers encourage, knowing their words impact others deeply. They don't create drama or seek to tear others down; instead, they point out the strengths of their friends and celebrate the wins in the lives of others.

- ☐ Peacemakers care, recognizing that empathy and compassion are powerful tools to connect with the people around them. They are curious about others, quick to listen, and slow to become angry.

Jesus, our peacemaker, resolved the war between eternal death and eternal life by sacrificing His life for all the grudges, wars, conflicts, arguments, and divisions that sin causes. By choosing to respond to God's calling to be a peacemaker, you can positively impact people with the message of unity in Christ. In a world in desperate need of harmony, your actions stand out. Through your choices, you can live your life in a way that warms others with the love of Christ.

11

1 Corinthians 1:31; 2 Corinthians 3:4–5
CONFIDENCE, NOT ARROGANCE

Years ago, my husband got me an Agent Carter mug that emphasized knowing your own worth regardless of the opinions of others.

Laughing, he gave it to me and told me that he loves how I am confident in my worth as a woman of God.

But even though my husband sees me as a confident woman, the truth is that I have insecurities. I'd venture a guess that all of us struggle with confidence to some degree.

While both genders experience struggles with self-confidence, our culture heaps impossible expectations on women. The world tells us we must be thin but not skinny, have perfect skin but not wear too much makeup, be accomplished but not look like we're trying too hard . . . The list goes on and on.

It can be difficult to understand how to be confident without dipping into arrogance. In my experience, young women often pull so far away from arrogance that they become too meek and submissive, allowing people to take them for granted and overlook their God-given talents.

Confidence comes from a belief in your worth, knowing that you are a beloved, forgiven child of the King. It's grounded in a positive view of who you are and the gifts God has blessed you with: your skills, passions, and opportunities. People who are confident are open to growth, appreciate others, and like to share their gifts with the world. They are caring teammates and can share their talents without putting others down.

Arrogance, on the other hand, stems from an inflated ego. An arrogant person believes she is better than others and frequently dismisses people's opinions. She resists growth and honest feedback and struggles to work collaboratively with others because she thinks she is superior.

Scripture tells us that the only talk that should come out of our mouths should be words shared about Jesus, our Savior, and what He has done for us. As 1 Corinthians 1:31 says,

> So that, as it is written, "Let the one
> who boasts, boast in the Lord."

In other words, our achievements should always point to God as the author of our abilities.

How do we act in a way that honors God and gives credit to the gifts He has bestowed upon us but does not allow arrogance to fill our hearts? The key is to remember the source of our confidence: Christ Jesus. Through Him, we have all we need and the calling to share what He has given us, in order that others may come to know His grace too.

As 2 Corinthians 3:4–5 reminds us,

Such is the confidence that we have through Christ toward God. Not that we are sufficient in ourselves to claim anything as coming from us, but our sufficiency is from God.

We can be confident in who we are, knowing that God has blessed us and has given us important gifts to share with our community. We don't need to ignore or underplay those gifts—they're from God!

As women living with confidence, we can celebrate and lift up other people too . . . just like my dear husband did.

Here's to you finding a mug—or something else special—to remind you to embrace your God-given worth.

Faith Notes

....
....
....
....
....
....
....
....
....
....
....
....

1

Genesis 50:20

REPURPOSE YOUR PAIN

I'm amazed at the way creative people repurpose old junk. From worn-out skateboards turned into lamps and abandoned desks made into trendy artwork, I love to see something broken be made new.

When it comes to people, the process of repurposing what is broken into something new isn't so easy though.

Our lives are often filled with circumstances we'd like to forget. Some of these experiences can haunt us for years, filling our hearts with regret, shame, or hurt. We don't want to be defined by these awful moments, and sometimes we stuff them down deep to try to forget. But what if God wants to use the very worst part of your story for His good?

You see, our God is a God of redemption. He transforms and heals, even when the odds seem impossible.

The Old Testament account of Joseph is a great example of God's power to repurpose pain. Joseph was the apple of his father's eye, but his brothers hated him for it. Their jealousy got out of hand, and they sold him into slavery. When Joseph got to a new land, Egypt, he was falsely accused and thrown in prison. Then his

God-given wisdom got him released from prison and placed in the second-highest position in Egypt. As part of his job, he worked to prevent people from starving to death in a famine—which saved Joseph's entire family too.

When Joseph encountered his brothers, seventeen years after they'd betrayed him, he spoke a powerful truth: "You meant evil against me, but God meant it for good, to bring it about that many people should be kept alive, as they are today" (Genesis 50:20).

In time and according to His plan for you, God can use your heartache for good too. No matter what mistakes and struggles you've faced, you may be shocked to find out how God repurposes the broken pieces of your life to create a work of art that inspires hope and healing for others.

Own your story, as messy as it may be. God can turn your mess into a message and your pain into an important purpose for His redemptive work to be on display to the world.

Faith Notes

....
....
....
....
....
....

2

Psalm 147:3

PICKING AT SCABS

I did a dumb thing during my freshman year of high school. Well, I did lots of dumb things, but this one stands out.

My friends and I were preparing for a pep rally for a home football game and decided to spray our hair with our school colors, green and gold. We stood outside on a chilly October afternoon, the temperature in central Minnesota already diving toward freezing.

I spent several minutes spraying my friends' hair, my index finger on the trigger of the aerosol can. Hair dye coated my finger and dripped down my palm, but I worked as quickly as I could. After I stopped, however, I realized that my finger was numb. Even after I warmed up inside, I couldn't feel anything.

Even worse, the skin on my index finger was white; it was completely dead.

It turns out that the cold weather and aerosol accelerated the process of frostbite. A visit to the doctor confirmed that the skin would "probably" grow back (not the comforting words you wanna hear), but it would take several months.

It did, indeed, take several months to heal. During that time, layers of dead skin slowly peeled off to reveal new growth underneath. It was an embarrassing, frustratingly long process.

I think back to my healing finger and remember all the scabby skin that grossed me out. It took everything in me not to keep picking at the scabs and allow it to heal properly. I felt like I might never be whole again.

While physical wounds like these are visible and give us a window in to the process of physical healing—however slow it may be—our emotional wounds often go unnoticed. We cannot see them as they fester and expand internally.

The good news is that Jesus sees the wounds in our soul. Psalm 147:3 reminds us,

He heals the brokenhearted and binds up their wounds.

Christ is our ultimate healer, removing the death sentence of sin and restoring us to an eternity of wholeness. And only He can completely heal our emotional wounds. His healing doesn't always happen overnight however. Recovery from soul wounds is often a marathon instead of a sprint. Just as my finger required lots of time and careful attention, our emotional hurts require the same.

Just as a physical wound might leave a scar on your body, your emotional healing might leave scars. But these scars are just another part of our story, reminding us that Christ alone makes us whole.

Invite Jesus to work on your heart, leading you through a journey of healing. Don't keep picking at scabs, but trust that Jesus is working something beautiful and new in you. Look to trusted professionals, family, and friends for support and guidance.

Even when the process feels slow, trust that God's timing is good. He is with you every step of the process, and in time, your renewed health will serve as a testimony of God's blessings in your life.

Faith Notes

....
....
....
....
....
....
....
....
....
....
....
....
....
....
....
....

3

Philippians 3:13–14

THE SHAME GAME

I'm a big sports fan, as many women are. Growing up in Chicago during the height of the Chicago Bulls championship era means that I'm a longtime fan and can rattle off a list of the players I watched dribble and shoot their way to victory.

I was always moved by the story of the team's star—one of the most famous basketball players in history—and how he overcame shame in his early years. Michael Jordan failed to make the varsity basketball team in high school, but instead of giving up, he doubled down on honing his skills. The next year, he won a spot on the varsity team and was eventually offered a basketball scholarship in college.

Against the odds, Jordan was drafted for the National Basketball Association, but he was soon criticized for not living up to the expectations that people put on him. He was labeled as a ball hog, and the weight of shame hung heavy on him.

Michael Jordan refused to play the shame game though. He used it to motivate himself to improve his skills and prioritize teamwork, two areas where he needed to grow.

Within a few years, he led his team to six championships and cemented himself as a legend in his field.

Jordan could have let his failure and embarrassment label him as a hopeless screw up. Instead, he believed there was life beyond his shame.

We may never be basketball superstars (although if you end up in the WNBA, I'll happily take courtside seats!), but we can let go of our own shame and embrace the newness that Jesus Christ gives us through His sacrifice on the cross.

One of the most famous figures in the New Testament is Paul, the man who persecuted and killed Christians before a miraculous conversion to faith in Jesus. He battled the power of shame in his own life, but he continued to proclaim to others that Christ's grace replaces our mistakes. In Philippians 3:13–14, he says,

> But one thing I do: forgetting what lies behind and straining forward to what lies ahead, I press on toward the goal for the prize of the upward call of God in Christ Jesus.

Paul's story reminds us that our shame doesn't define us. It cannot hold us back from what God has in store. The past may have written an embarrassing story, but Christ's forgiveness allows you to begin your next chapter with a fresh start.

4

John 20:24–29; Isaiah 55:8–9
DEALING WITH DOUBT

We sat in a circle, everyone silent. Finally, I spoke. "You know, it's normal to struggle with your faith and have doubts and questions about God. I still have plenty of questions, even as a youth leader, and things don't always make perfect sense to me."

Suddenly, the mood in the room shifted. Students started talking over each other, confessing that they struggled with these same things in their faith walk.

Instead of the quiet, apprehensive group, I was surrounded by teens who were opening up about their lives. My being honest and admitting that I struggle with doubt sometimes gave them permission to be honest too.

For some reason, people get really nervous talking about doubt, even though we find plenty of insight about it in Scripture. The way I see it, if you're really using your brain and thinking deeply about your faith in Jesus, you're probably going to have questions, concerns, and things that you just don't understand. Just as God met each struggling, questioning, doubting person in the Bible, He meets your curious soul. He knows your heart and knows that you earnestly seek the truth. Our doubts can never discount who God is and what He does.

When we recognize that doubt is a natural part of our growth and that we aren't alone in experiencing it, we can approach Jesus more honestly. Read the accounts of Moses and Jonah, Job and Peter, and plenty of other notable figures to see how they doubted God's direction, questioned His promptings, and fought against His will. Yet God still used them to accomplish His purpose.

I've always identified with "doubting Thomas," who questioned Jesus' resurrection until he saw Jesus' wounds with his own eyes (John 20:24–29). Jesus didn't treat Thomas with disgust or contempt. He understood his doubts and provided undeniable proof.

Isaiah 55:8–9 reminds us,

> For My thoughts are not your thoughts, neither are your ways My ways, declares the LORD. For as the heavens are higher than the earth, so are My ways higher than your ways and My thoughts than your thoughts.

God's wisdom surpasses ours. Our Creator, who knows every hair on our head and every thought in our minds, is well aware of the doubts we hold—and He wants us to engage with Him for answers.

When you struggle with doubt, don't hide it from God. Look to Scripture for answers, spend time in prayer, and talk to trusted adults about your questions. Consider your doubts as an opportunity to grow in a more genuine relationship with God, knowing that He will meet your every wondering with love. In your journal, write down questions you have been struggling with.

5

Psalm 118:8–9; 1 Corinthians 2:5
DISENTANGLING

Have you heard the term *deconstruction*?

It's a popular sentiment in the faith community lately. It refers to the process of critically examining your spiritual beliefs to deal with questions and doubts, and it often involves assessing the doctrines or practices of your religious tradition.

While the practice of deconstruction is a personal journey that helps some find deeper, more authentic faith, others may decide to leave their religious community or find a different belief system.

One of the common topics that comes up for those working through deconstruction is how the church has caused many problems throughout history. While the Christian Church has shared the saving message of the Gospel and helped untold billions of people, it's true that it has also been a source of problems and pain for many. Abuse, neglect, power struggles, and corruption have tainted even well-intentioned faith communities.

Why is this? It's because people are sinful by nature, and our sin infects even the most sacred spaces. Because the real issue here is mankind, not God, I think a more accurate term to use is *disentangling* what people have added to the church rather than blaming God for the mess.

Martin Luther, the famous sixteenth-century reformer, went through a process of disentangling what Scripture actually proclaimed about Jesus from what the Catholic Church was teaching at that time. As he intently studied God's Word to find the truth and went public with what the church had incorrectly added, he faced persecution and death threats. Ultimately, he was kicked out of the church, yet rather than grow disillusioned with the church, he doubled down on studying what God says in His Word. The result: Luther's faith in Christ and in salvation through Him grew stronger than ever.

Psalm 118:8–9 reminds us,

> It is better to take refuge in the LORD than to trust in man. It is better to take refuge in the LORD than to trust in princes.

Likewise, 1 Corinthians 2:5 contains Paul's insight that our faith does not rest on human wisdom but on God's power:

> So that your faith might not rest in the wisdom of men but in the power of God.

When people fail you, look to God's steadfast, unchanging character.

When you wonder about your spiritual life, turn to the Word of God and find truth, power, and peace.

When you encounter disappointing things within the church or Christian community, look beyond human flaws and see God's unconditional love. He transcends the shortcomings of human institutions and offers us true security.

As you grow in faith, keep your focus on our God, who will never fail you. In Him, you'll find the steadfast grace and truth that earthly relationships may lack.

Faith Notes

....
....
....
....
....
....
....
....
....
....
....
....
....
....
....
....
....
....
....
....

6

Psalm 106:1; 1 John 4:16
GRATITUDE

A few months ago, I was on a flight that experienced turbulence so bad that the plane couldn't land. I've experienced a lot of turbulence from the frequent flying I do, but never any as bone jarring as what I felt on that flight. Nearly half of the people on the plane vomited into the seat-back paper bags as our pilots made multiple attempts to land the aircraft. Even the flight attendants were crying as they announced that we were in an emergency situation. The plane finally landed, and I've never experienced more gratitude for a pilot. I enthusiastically thanked both of them for their expert ability to guide our plane to the ground in such difficult circumstances.

Being grateful is a state of mind. When we tune in to what we appreciate, our focus shifts from what we lack to what we have, giving us a greater sense of contentment and happiness. By choosing to focus on blessings instead of struggles, we can soothe our anxious souls and remember that God is good and takes excellent care of us. As Psalm 106:1 proclaims,

> Praise the LORD! Oh give thanks to the LORD, for He is good, for His steadfast love endures forever!

When we live in the knowledge that God's love endures forever, our minds can rest easy in this foundation of security that our Savior's love for us provides. 1 John 4:16 assures us:

So we have come to know and to believe the love that God has for us. God is love, and whoever abides in love abides in God, and God abides in him.

Reflect on three things you're thankful that God has given you. Choose to live with a sense of gratitude, asking the Holy Spirit to give you eyes to see the blessings all around you. As you continue to cultivate a grateful heart, you'll find that gratitude is a gift that keeps on giving.

Activity

Have a gratitude scavenger hunt with your family or friends. Next time you have dinner together, invite everyone to bring food items in the following colors—orange, green, yellow, blue, and red—as reminders of your daily blessings. As you look at the different hues, go through the following list and take turns thanking Jesus out loud for these things in your life.

- ☐ Orange: a person you're thankful for

- ☐ Green: a place you're thankful for

- ☐ Yellow: a food you're thankful for

- ☐ Blue: something that starts with the first letter of your name that you're thankful for

- ☐ Red: a place you're thankful for

7
Mark 10:45
THE SERVANT

Have you ever had a friend who's ambitious to the point of annoyance?

I can't read the account of James and John, vying for their seats at Jesus' right and left sides, without feeling irritated. Who did these guys think they were? Their self-importance oozes through in Mark 10.

As the disciples squabbled about James's and John's desire to outrank the rest of them, Jesus reminded them that true greatness comes from humility. Read His words in Mark 10:45:

> For even the Son of Man came not to be served but to serve, and to give His life as a ransom for many.

Jesus sought no pedestal. He lived to serve others and give up His life so we could live. That's the kind of attitude we're called to emulate. Our character as Christians is a valuable witness to the world. What character traits did Jesus embody? Obedience. Humility. Service. Love. Compassion. Grace. Encouragement.

In college, one of my art classes required me to tour a museum. I found myself walking around with a classmate I didn't know well. As we studied paintings and sculptures, he asked me about myself. When I shared that I was a Christian, he visibly reeled back.

Over the next hour, my classmate bombarded me with his spiritual wrestlings. We ended up seated in front of a large painting, where he turned to me and said, "You're the only Christian I've ever met who didn't beat me over the head with your beliefs. So what exactly do you believe, anyway?"

As we sat together, surrounded by museum visitors, I shared the Gospel with him.

The way we live out our faith and the way we treat those around us matters. Approaching others with the same attitude of Jesus opens doors.

A reminder of forgiveness exists within this account of James and John too, where Jesus lovingly refocuses the disciples on what truly matters. On the days when we live arrogantly, fail to extend compassion and choose not to serve each other, God's grace still envelops us.

The sacrifice of Jesus, the Servant, echoes through eternity.

Questions

- ☐ What quality of Jesus do you admire most?

- ☐ Where do you struggle most to display a heart modeled after Jesus?

- ☐ Where are you tempted to focus on achievement rather than on emulating Christ?

8

John 8:11

GO AND SIN NO MORE

A re you protective of what's in the search history of your phone or computer? Most of us are. Whether you're hiding the fact that you've been searching for answers to an embarrassing problem or that you've been looking at something you're not supposed to be viewing, the thought of someone uncovering our private queries can be terrifying and humiliating.

The New Testament shares the story of a woman who felt these same emotions as she was dragged out into a crowd after being caught in an act of adultery. The woman's accusers dragged her in front of Jesus and demanded that she be judged for her mistakes. By law, she deserved to be stoned to death.

Yet Jesus refused to meet her mistake with condemnation. He told the crowd that anyone who was blameless could throw the first stone. One by one, the members of the crowd disappeared, aware of their own guilt. Jesus then extended compassion. As John 8:11 recounts, Jesus told the woman,

Neither do I condemn you; go, and from now on sin no more.

The adulterous woman had been caught in the act. She was definitely guilty. But in Jesus' refusal to condemn her, we see the incredible gift of forgiveness extended to someone who'd messed up. This is the same forgiveness that Jesus offers to us.

As God the Son, Jesus knows the secret sins we commit, even when those sins stay hidden. Because we are God's children, we are called to a higher standard. God gives guidelines (the Commandments) to guide our behavior and guard us against hurting ourselves. That's because He loves us and wants what's best for our lives.

We aren't very good at following these laws though. We make mistakes; sometimes our sins are deliberate. Sin separates us from God, who is holy. What is unholy can't even be in His presence. But Jesus steps in, removes our sin, and restores us to God.

Likewise, Jesus stepped in for the woman caught in adultery. His perfection covered her imperfection. During this encounter, Jesus reminded everyone else who was present that they were sinners too. Unlike the woman, these other people ducked their heads and went away. They tried to hide. When Jesus told her to "go, and from now on sin no more," He gave her a fresh start to move forward, forgiven and made new.

Do you have a secret sinful habit or past? Jesus has already forgiven you. Embrace this! Hold your head up, "go, and from now on sin no more." God knows you aren't perfect, but He wants you to embrace the forgiveness He offers and allow it to change your heart.

9

Mark 8:34–36

THE ROLLER COASTER OF SPIRITUAL LIFE

Apprehension. Uncertainty. Confusion.

Have you felt these emotions lately?

I've wrestled with them plenty of times. When I moved to Houston a few years ago, taking a new work position in the midst of a global pandemic, I found myself carried away with these feelings.

Sometimes we find ourselves swept onto a path that's unexpected. It might be the sudden loss of a friendship or loved one. It could be a blessing like a scholarship or a job offer, or it might be a burden like a health scare or a financial strain.

Jesus Himself was the definition of the unexpected. He didn't appear triumphantly but instead humbled Himself to be made man, born of a woman the same way everyone else is, and live a fully human life. He endured the humility of childhood, learning to feed and dress Himself though He is the bread of life and the creator of the universe.

Mark 8 shares a meaningful story from Jesus' life, when He took time to quietly teach His disciples, away from the crowds. Why would Jesus pull away from the crowd and spend time with only those closest to Him? At times, Jesus focused specifically on His followers. He knew how hard their jobs would be and how crucial it was to equip them to carry on once He ascended to heaven.

To me, these verses indicate that the process of spiritual growth isn't a quick journey. It takes time, intentionality, and dedication to what matters most. The disciples needed to learn to put aside their duties in order to focus on and learn from Jesus. He modeled it for them, through the choice He made to spend time with them.

In Mark 8:34–36, Jesus tells His followers that lives entwined with His will involve intentionality:

> And calling the crowd to Him with His disciples, He said to them, "If anyone would come after Me, let him deny himself and take up his cross and follow Me. For whoever would save his life will lose it, but whoever loses his life for My sake and the gospel's will save it. For what does it profit a man to gain the whole world and forfeit his soul?"

Like those disciples, we are singled out, chosen to follow Jesus. We are given faith to know this and to do this. And to follow Jesus means trusting that He is our Savior and we are His redeemed children. That's our identity. As a wise friend once told me, "What matters most is not what you do but who you are."

When I pry my eyes from my to-do list, I find comfort in the moments I spend in Scripture. The Holy

Spirit speaks what I need every day, whether it is peace, encouragement, wisdom, or admonition.

Here, I find the constant reminders, too, of who I am. It's not about what I do but about who God has created me to be.

Jesus saved us through sacrifice, not through pomp and circumstance. What a powerful reminder that God so often works in ways we don't expect.

When we're caught up in the unanticipated, dealing with fear and anxiety, worrying about our futures, let us focus on the voice of Jesus, who calls us to spend time with Him, hearing His words for us recorded in the Bible. Even in the moments that surprise us, we can be confident that His death and resurrection change our apprehension, uncertainty, and confusion into hope.

Questions:

- ☐ In what aspect of your life are you feeling worry, uncertainty, or anxiety right now? Write or speak those things aloud, confessing to Jesus that you need His presence in your life.

- ☐ In what situations do you struggle to remember that you as a person matter more than what you do and accomplish?

- ☐ The Holy Spirit often works in unexpected ways, even when things seem challenging. What are three unexpected blessings you've experienced this week?

10

Psalm 103:2; Ephesians 5:20
COUNTING YOUR BLESSINGS

It hit me one morning as I looked out the window at the sunny blue sky and a day filled with unlimited potential: How many sunrises have I seen in my life? When I did the math, I was floored. To date, I've experienced more than 13,000 mornings. That's a lot of days to enjoy!

In the hectic rush of our lives, it's easy to overlook the many blessings that surround us. Psalm 103:2 tells us,

> Bless the LORD, O my soul, and forget not all His benefits.

And Ephesians 5:20 reminds us that we are to be

> Giving thanks always and for everything to God the Father in the name of our Lord Jesus Christ.

Spend some time today counting your blessings. When we reflect on God's many gifts, our perspective can be transformed to be more positive and grateful. Consider finding answers to the following questions to see how richly blessed you are. In your lifetime,

- ☐ how many sunrises have you experienced?

- ☐ how many heartbeats have you had? (An average person's heart beats 80 times in a minute.)

- how many miles have you walked? (An average person has a stride length of approximately 2.5 feet. That means that it takes more than 2,000 steps to walk a mile; 10,000 steps would be almost 5 miles.)

- how many meals have you consumed?

- how many weekends have you enjoyed?

- how many gallons of water have you consumed? (An average person drinks a half-gallon each day.)

- how many houses have you lived in so far?

- how many cars have you driven?

- how much time have you spent on technology? (An average teenager currently spends six to nine hours a day on technology.)

- how many hours of education have you received?

- how much time have you spent in church?

Even when times are challenging, there's clearly something to be thankful for each day. First and foremost? Jesus came for you, died for you, and rose again for you. May God give you eyes to see the blessings He's given you and a grateful heart to thank Him for them.

Faith Notes

....
....
....
....

1

Matthew 6:25–30
ANXIETY ABOUT THE FUTURE

Virtually every woman I speak with, young and old, knows the feeling of anxiety gripping her heart. Perhaps you're concerned about a test or difficult conversation looming on the horizon. Or maybe you're heartsick over a loved one's health or worried about your own future.

Do anxious thoughts race through your brain even as you read this?

A wise person once compared worry to a rocking chair: it gives you something to do, but you're not going anywhere. Likewise, we know anxiety is an unhelpful emotion, but we can't always help ourselves from falling into its trap.

Jesus understands how we feel when we're anxious. In Matthew 6:25–30, we are reminded that God values us more than anything else in creation. Just as He takes care of the birds and flowers, He makes sure we have all that we need in this life:

Therefore I tell you, do not be anxious about your life, what you will eat or what you will drink, nor about your body, what you will put on. Is not life more than food, and the body more than clothing? Look at the birds of the air: they neither sow nor reap nor gather into barns, and yet your heavenly Father feeds them. Are you not of more valuable than they?

And which of you by being anxious can add
a single hour to his span of life?

And why are you anxious about clothing? Consider the lilies of the field, how they grow: they neither toil nor spin, yet I tell you, even Solomon in all his glory was not arrayed like one of these.

But if God so clothes the grass of the field, which today is alive and tomorrow is thrown into the oven, will he not much more clothe you, O you of little faith?

Trust that your Creator knows you better than you even know yourself and that He knows every challenge and blessing ahead of you.

When anxiety grabs you in a chokehold, whisper to yourself that there's no need to worry because God is in control of this world and your future. You are safe in the hands of the One who loves you, forgives you, and secures your future with Him in heaven.

Activity

Without taking time to overthink it, brainstorm a list of all the things that make you anxious. Pause, and offer up these worries to Jesus. Spend a few quiet moments in prayer, then jot down a few of the blessings that come to mind as you think about all the comfort and joy that Christ offers to you.

2

1 Corinthians 6:19–20

TAKING CARE OF YOURSELF

In the early weeks of the pandemic, as my youth group shifted entirely online, I was hosting Zoom meetings all day long to connect with people.

In the middle of dealing with my own worry and attempts to find toilet paper, which had mostly disappeared from store shelves, I was counseling anxious teens every single day. For a while, there wasn't a day that passed without someone sobbing on my screen.

I was exhausted and mentally depleted but still trying to care for others. One day, after a Zoom session with my high school girls' group, one of the students stuck around after everyone else left the chat.

"Hey, how are you doing?" Olivia asked, concern evident in her voice. "I just realized that you're constantly caring for everyone else but that no one is asking you how you're handling this."

In that moment, the tears started to cascade down my face. Olivia was right: I was pouring every bit of energy into everyone else without receiving anything back.

In the commotion of life, it's easy to forget the importance of taking care of yourself. Yet, our bodies are gifts from God, and He has entrusted us with the responsibility of caring for our mental, emotional, and physical well-being. We read in 1 Corinthians 6:19–20,

> Do you not know that your body is a temple of the Holy Spirit within you, whom you have from God? You are not your own, for you were bought with a price. So glorify God in your body.

Taking care of yourself isn't selfish. It's acknowledging the gift of self that God has given you and doing what is necessary to preserve the body in which His Holy Spirit dwells. Self-care is an act of stewardship.

Make sure you take time to care for yourself by eating healthy foods and exercising your body and brain. Get enough sleep (which is especially important for teenage bodies!), unplug regularly from the online world, and take care of your mental health.

If you feel overwhelmed or emotional, open up to trusted friends and adults about your feelings. Not only does the Bible recommend the benefits of community but there's also a lot of research in the scientific world about how connection positively impacts our lives and health.

When you take care of the body God has given you, you honor your Creator. You acknowledge that you are important to Him. So important, in fact, that He made it possible for you to not only have a life and purpose here but also an eternal life with Him, through Jesus.

Write down two things you can do this week to take care of yourself to honor your Creator.

3

2 Corinthians 12:9

PERFECTION'S UNRELENTING PRESSURE

In high school, I agonized over achieving the perfect "beach hair." It had to look effortlessly cool, though it took a ridiculous amount of washing, blow drying, curling, and brushing to get the look just right. I wanted it to look natural, but it was a stressful, demanding process. Eventually, I abandoned my attempt to manipulate my tresses into something they could never be. "My hair is flat and straight," I said to the mirror. "I give up."

Just as my attempt at beach hair was unrealistic, the idea of effortless perfection is a lie on many levels.

Everything we do requires effort—there's no such thing as having an effortless life. And perfection? It isn't realistic. As hard as we try, we'll always be sinful people who mess up, make mistakes, and face setbacks.

Seeking perfection will always be chasing a goal that continues to elude us, no matter how hard we try to achieve it. The trap of perfection is particularly tempting for women. The world around us has conflicting expectations for us: we should be sweet, but also speak up for ourselves and be bold. We should be in control of our emotions, but not unemotional and cold. We should be perfectly dressed and behaved, but we can't look like we've tried too hard or we're too self focused. We should be confident, but never arrogant. We should be popular and well loved, but we can't let our guard down and show our imperfections.

In contrast to society's toxic demands of perfection, Jesus invites us to simply be real. He knows that we're imperfect. He knows about our bad breath, our bad moods, and the bad words we say. And He loves us deeply, despite all these flaws.

The apostle Paul found comfort in this truth of being accepted for who he was, without needing to be perfect. As he wrote in 2 Corinthians 12:9,

> But He said to me, "My grace is sufficient for you, for My power is made perfect in weakness." Therefore I will boast all the more gladly of my weaknesses, so that the power of Christ may rest upon me.

With Jesus, we never have to pretend to be anything other than who we really are: imperfect, but still perfectly loved, children of God covered with Christ's grace.

Activity

Use a whiteboard marker to write the words "Imperfect, but perfectly loved by Jesus" on your bathroom mirror. As you get ready for the day, remind yourself that Jesus knows exactly who you are and loves you, even when you make mistakes and fail. Leave it up as long as you need the reminder!

4

Psalm 34:18
EMOTIONAL ROLLER COASTER

For a summer, I worked a high-speed roller coaster at Universal Studios in Orlando. Though the heat caused sweat to trickle down my uniform at all hours of the day, I loved watching people's faces as they strapped in to the roller coaster.

Some people couldn't stop smiling as they clung to the handlebars, excited about the twists and turns ahead. Others had furrowed brows and compressed lips, apprehensive about the ride. Then there were some people who had completely blank faces, displaying neither joy nor fear about being launched sixty miles per hour down a metal track and looping upside down.

Life feels a lot like a roller coaster of emotions as you encounter unexpected twists, turns, and barrel rolls. While emotions are a beautiful part of being human, they can sometimes feel overwhelming.

It's normal to feel a range of emotions, from frustration and despair to elation and excitement. Our Creator intended for us to feel deeply and experience emotion.

Keep in mind that your emotions tend to be more extreme as you encounter everything that's changing in your body and brain, your relationships with your parents and peers, and the routines of daily life. It's common for young people to have more intense emotional experiences and to speed between extremes . . . just like a roller coaster.

As you find yourself dealing with emotions, remember the words of Psalm 34:18:

> The LORD is near to the brokenhearted
> and saves the crushed in spirit.

In the moments when you struggle most, don't forget that God is compassionate, He is with you, and He holds you close. Your emotions don't scare Him off, nor do your emotions define you. Your identity is tethered to Christ, your Savior, and His love and strength will sustain you through the days when you're stuck in your feels.

Faith Notes

....
....
....
....
....
....
....
....
....

5

Joshua 1:9
ALONE AND AFRAID

I jolted awake to the sound of furious barking from Ella, the dog who'd been snoozing at my feet until that moment.

From just outside my open bedroom window, I could hear thrashing from the bushes.

I yanked back the sheets and grabbed a flashlight. Through the window, I scanned the bushes, Ella growling behind me, but I couldn't see anything. After several minutes, I lay back down, but my heart was hammering in my chest, and I couldn't go back to sleep. Wild pigs commonly broke into the yard. Was that the source of the noise?

I was house sitting in Hawaii by myself (well, by myself with Ella) for a week. That night, I unlocked a new fear: loneliness.

As I lay in the dark, I realized how far away I was from all my friends and family. I was in a remote part of the Big Island, dog sitting Ella, with a huge ocean between me and everyone I knew. I couldn't even call anyone. The time difference prevented me from reaching out to hear a familiar voice for comfort.

Loneliness often strikes us unexpectedly. Whether you experience a tragedy, have a falling out with someone, or are physically distanced from others, the pain of isolation can be disconcerting or even overwhelming.

In those moments when you feel alone, be assured that God holds you in His palm. Although I couldn't physically see Him that night, I knew immense peace as I prayed and brought my fear to Jesus. In time, I was able to drift off to sleep and know that I was safe and loved.

Joshua 1:9 shares a powerful truth about how God is with us, no matter what:

Have I not commanded you? Be strong and courageous.
Do not be frightened, and do not be dismayed, for
the LORD your God is with you wherever you go.

No matter if it's wild pigs that scare you at night or if being alone in the middle of a crowd unnerves you, your Savior is right there with you. Yes, there are dangers in this world, but be assured that Jesus overcame evil for you. Go to Him with your worries and fears, and receive the peace and comfort that He always gives.

Activity

In the daytime, write down a few favorite Bible verses that remind you that Jesus is with you no matter what. Put this list next to your bed. Before you fall asleep, take a look at these verses and remind yourself that you are God's beloved child. If you happen to wake up in the middle of the night, meditate on these verses again and talk to God from the quietness of your bedroom.

6

Deuteronomy 31:6
A DANGEROUS WORLD

My student's text stopped me cold; I was frozen with concern.

"My school is under lockdown with an active shooter," she messaged.

I didn't know what to do. Respond and risk her phone dinging? Give advice on how to protect herself? Call her parents and see if they knew anything more? Go to the school to see if I could help?

As my mind filled with worry, I turned to Jesus, knowing He could interpret the jumbled thoughts in my head. I certainly couldn't put my feelings into words in that moment.

Thank God that the lockdown ended quickly and no one was hurt.

Yet, the shadow of fear persisted for the students at this high school, as it does for many young people all over the world. The constant concern for one's safety is real, and it can make it hard for some to trust anyone they meet or any place they go. It might surprise you that a lot of adults struggle to understand this worry because it wasn't a part of their own childhood.

Maybe you feel like it's a lonely burden that people don't seem to understand.

Whether you've been traumatized by experiencing this kind of threat yourself or watched a friend, family member, or other community face tragedy, it can be hard to process the complex emotions.

You may feel anger, guilt, grief, confusion, anxiety, hatred, and regret. You may rage against the killers who perpetrate senseless acts of violence, or you may become angry with the lack of security measures and poor responses to tragedy. You may worry constantly that you'll experience a terrifying situation yourself and feel the weight of always looking over your shoulder wherever you are, whether it's a classroom or a concert.

In those moments when worry and fear fill your mind, turn to Jesus' promises of love, hope, and protection. As Deuteronomy 31:6 reminds us,

> Be strong and courageous. Do not fear or be in dread of them, for it is the LORD your God who goes with you. He will not leave you or forsake you.

No matter what terrible, tragic things we encounter in this sinful world, our almighty God is stronger and more powerful than all evil. Although our souls may be heavy because of what we face, God goes with us, never abandoning us to face these things alone. Remember that Jesus defeated evil once and for all. Bad things still happen on earth, but you belong to Jesus, and He protects your soul for eternity. Let Him be your source of comfort in this broken world.

Activity

Come up with a phrase of your own to use every time you feel fear creeping in. Maybe it's something like, "Protect me, Jesus" or "Be with me, Lord." Recite it to yourself every day when you feel worry, and let it be a reminder to you that God is with you in every moment.

....
....
....
....
....
....
....
....
....
....
....
....
....
....
....
....
....
....
....

1

Psalm 119:9, 37

CONSUMED BY WHAT WE CONSUME

As a young adult, I worked at a clothing store. I've always loved fashion, and this job allowed me to discover how much I enjoyed styling outfits for customers.

I was surprised to learn that working in retail had a profoundly negative effect on me, however. Being around beautiful clothes and talking about outfits with customers every day was making me obsessed with my appearance. Almost overnight, all I could think about was styling outfits and what cute accessories I could buy with my employee discount. I had to talk myself out of spending every paycheck on new clothes.

While your obsession might not be the same as mine was, the truth is that we're often consumed by what we consume. So what is it that you're spending all your brain power thinking about? Are you obsessed with tracking your favorite social media star? Do you fill your waking hours with homework, trying to be the top of your class? Are you overly connected to your friends or boyfriend? Is your identity all about a sport or hobby?

We live in a world where our obsessions can be fed constantly. In the confines of the internet and our cell phones, we have access to unprecedented amounts of toxicity. While many of these things are not bad in and of themselves, with all the consuming we're doing, we sometimes forget to pay attention to our heavenly Father.

Throughout the Bible, God reminds us that our minds can lead us down problematic pathways unless they are tethered firmly in Him.

> How can a young man keep his way pure? By guarding it according to Your word. (Psalm 119:9)

By continuing to ground ourselves in Scripture, a faith community, and the grace received through the Lord's Supper, we can better withstand the troublesome temptations of the world.

In a world that tempts us to be consumed with shallow things like celebrities, clothes, gaming, and reputation, Christ is our anchor to remind us that we are set apart as His treasured children. May Psalm 119:37 be a frequent prayer for you as you consider what you consume:

> Turn my eyes from looking at worthless things; and give me life in Your ways.

Next time you put on an outfit, spend a moment looking at yourself in the mirror. Remind yourself of how God sees you: as His forgiven, beloved child who is clothed in Christ and has an inheritance in heaven.

In your journal, express your gratitude to Christ for covering you in His perfect righteousness.

2
Psalm 51:10
TOO FAR

I got the call early in the morning. I picked up, my brain still foggy, and heard someone crying on the other end.

As I listened, the young woman sobbed out the story of all the mistakes she'd made the night before. A combination of too much alcohol and a pushy guy had resulted in her doing things she was ashamed to share. "I'm not that kind of girl!" she cried, regret evident in her words.

I wish I could say that this was the only conversation like this that I've ever had, but that wouldn't be true. It's a frequent one. One of the most common confessions I hear from young women is despair over how they've been pushed outside of their comfort zone to do something they regret.

Whether it's going too far with a guy, doing something stupid as their friends egged them on, getting hooked on a negative habit, or trying something they know is wrong, many of the teens I know have seriously messed up.

When we cross lines we know we shouldn't, we often become filled with despair and shame. We know we've messed up, and we don't know how to make things right.

The good news for your regret-filled heart is that you've never gone too far for God. No matter what mistakes you've made—what you've looked at online, what you've sampled, or what you've done with someone—God offers you forgiveness through the sacrifice of His Son, Jesus Christ, on the cross.

Psalm 51:10 says,

> Create in me a clean heart, O God, and
> renew a right spirit within me.

These words are a beautiful statement of repentance. And while we can't undo mistakes already committed, Jesus offers us a fresh start.

Where there is hurt and shame, He creates a clean heart. Your sins are forgiven and no longer held against you. You don't need to live under the shadow of a bad reputation or let guilt consume you. While the ramifications of your mistakes may continue, your identity in Christ is secure. He covers you with a mantle of His grace and steers you toward a future filled with hope.

No matter what you've done, you're still a child of the King. The Bible is packed with accounts of all sorts of people who made massive mistakes. Those accounts are there so we can be assured that God used these people to accomplish His will, and He will continue to use your life to accomplish His important purpose.

Read through the account of David in Psalms and see how God used this sinful man for His glory–even when David royally screwed up.

Just like David, you're never too far gone for God to use you. You are never too far out of His reach for Him to hold you. Nothing you do will separate you from your Savior.

You'll never ever be too far gone for Him to stop loving you.

Faith Notes

....
....
....
....
....
....
....
....
....
....
....
....
....
....
....
....

3

Exodus 32; Colossians 3:12–17
IDOLS

I once dated a guy who was obsessed with the vintage Mustang he owned. He babied this car, driving it carefully and working on it all the time. When he wasn't driving it, he talked about it . . . nonstop.

One time, I joked to him that his Mustang was his idol. He didn't contradict me, unfortunately.

Anything in our lives can become an idol when it demands our affection and attention. It might be a relationship, possession, sport, or lifestyle—anything we find ourselves lusting after.

In the Old Testament, the Israelites turned to the golden calf even after God had miraculously saved their lives. Exodus 32 tells how God's people strayed from Him and attempted to find purpose in a statue.

Idols aren't just golden statues though—they're anything we put above God in our hearts. Idols distract our attention from the God who created us and saved us. The object of our attention may not be bad in and of itself. Often, these objects are good things, which makes it really tricky to discern idols in our lives.

In order to figure out if something has become an idol to you, be honest and ask yourself what you're giving the most attention and affection to. Consider what you daydream about or talk about the most, or what you worry about losing more than anything else. Identify what you think about before you fall asleep at night and when you wake in the morning.

Young people can be especially vulnerable to idols as they learn to navigate life's challenges. To counteract this temptation, connect with God regularly by reading His Word, praying in Jesus' name, attending worship, and receiving the Lord's Supper. None of these things takes much time, and each of them benefits you with strengthened faith and assurance of forgiveness. In addition, consider talking with trusted friends or family members about your struggles and ask them to help you see the bigger picture.

What should we be paying attention to, instead of earthly idols? Colossians 3:12–17 is a great guide for us:

Put on then, as God's chosen ones, holy and beloved, compassionate hearts, kindness, humility, meekness, and patience, bearing with one another and, if one has a complaint against another, forgiving each other; as the Lord has forgiven you, so you also must forgive. And above all these put on love, which binds everything together in perfect harmony. And let the peace of Christ rule in your hearts, to which indeed you were called in one body. And be thankful. Let the word of Christ dwell in you richly, teaching and admonishing one another in all wisdom, singing psalms and hymns and spiritual songs, with thankfulness in your hearts to God. And whatever you do, in word or deed, do everything in the name of the Lord Jesus, giving thanks to God the Father through Him.

Even when we find ourselves grappling with something we idolize, God doesn't walk away from us in disgust. He reminds us to take our idols off the pedestal and put Him at the center of our lives.

He is always eager to welcome us back as His beloved children, even when we forget that that's who we are.

Faith Notes

....
....
....
....
....
....
....
....
....
....
....
....
....

1

Ephesians 6:2–3
HONORING YOUR PARENTS

A few years ago, I was cleaning out my childhood room and I found homework from my mom.

In response to my bad behavior, my mother had punished me by assigning writing a two-page paper on how I needed to adjust my negative attitude. She had a deadline and everything, and she actually graded it.

I mean, I give her props for a creative punishment.

The Bible has a lot to say about respecting other people and puts extra importance on how we are to respect and honor our parents. Ephesians 6:2–3 reminds us,

> "Honor your father and mother" (this is the first commandment with a promise), "that it may go well with you and that you may live long in the land."

Did you catch it? Honoring your parents is linked to the promise of blessings. When we extend respect and love to our parents, it leads to an enjoyable, long life.

Also, it probably leads to fewer essays you'll have to write about your bad behavior.

What does this respect look like? It looks like viewing your parents through the lens of grace, understanding that they are imperfect people who need forgiveness. It's about being obedient and honoring their wishes and valuing their wisdom even if it doesn't make sense to you. It's about acknowledging their sacrifices on your behalf and showing an interest in their lives.

It's not always smooth sailing in your relationships with your parents. Conflict and clashing are an inevitable part of growing up. Think of yourself as a little baby bird, comfy and tucked into a tiny nest. The older you get, the more you start to outgrow that nest. As you're crammed in there with the rest of your family, you start bumping into each other more often and ruffling each other's feathers.

In time, there just isn't room for you and your parents to be sharing that nest anymore . . . and that's good! It means you've grown up and you're ready to fly on your own, soaring into new adventures with their support and love.

But maybe your situation isn't like that. Some people (maybe you) don't have both parents in the same house. Sometimes parents don't live up to their role as responsible adults.

No matter your situation, try not to let the bumps and frustrations take away from the fact that God has blessed you where you are. After all, putting you in this place at this time is God's plan for you, for your family, and for the world around you. Your heavenly Father made you His child in your Baptism and promises you a home in heaven with Him. Let the way you treat your parents reflect your gratitude for this gift and remember that honoring your parents is God's path for you to enjoy a fulfilling and blessed life.

Activity

What's one thing you could do today to bless your parents or siblings? Maybe it's making a favorite dessert to surprise them, tidying up the living room, or writing them a short note of appreciation. Get creative in showing that you're thankful for the family God has blessed you with!

....
....
....
....
....
....
....
....
....
....
....
....
....
....
....
....
....
....

2

Ecclesiastes 4:9–10; Romans 8:17
SIBLING RIVALRY

I winced in pain, drawing on every ounce of self-discipline to keep from crying out. My little brother grinned, then held out his hand. I flicked him as hard as I could and watched his face crumple in agony.

Sure, playing bloody knuckles during church isn't the best thing to be doing. But in our younger years, my brother, Chase, and I bonded through attempting to beat each other up. Chase and I now look back fondly on the times we shared in our childhood, whether they were good or bad. We teased each other, pulled pranks together, and drove our parents nuts.

If you have siblings or stepsiblings of your own, you know that peculiar love-hate bond you share. Siblings are a special gift—not only to help us deal with our parents' uniqueness but also to be lifelong friends and allies.

Ecclesiastes 4:9–10 underscores the importance of community in our lives:

> Two are better than one, because they have a good
> reward for their toil. For if they fall, one will lift
> up his fellow. But woe to him who is alone when
> he falls and has not another to lift him up!

Siblings share your inside jokes, know your family history and quirks, and get you in a way that no one else can. While it's natural to get under each other's skin and fight, your siblings are an important support during the difficult moments of life. I'm always amazed at how even the most distant siblings can draw close together in tough times, like facing tragedy and death together.

Whenever you're around other people long enough, you're bound to experience conflict and disagreements. Remember that your siblings are a gift from God to help you through life, and you're intended to help them too. Our siblings can help us learn the reality that this world isn't perfect, that conflict and frustration are one of the results of the fall of mankind in the Garden of Eden (remember siblings Cain and Abel?). Here's the most important thing: along with our siblings, we are children of God,

And if children, then heirs—heirs of God and fellow heirs with Christ, provided we suffer with Him in order that we may also be glorified with Him. (Romans 8:17)

By keeping this truth at the forefront of your mind, you can work through even the most frustrating circumstances with empathy and forgiveness.

The next time you play bloody knuckles with a sibling, spend a moment thanking God for the gift of this lifelong friend. Cherish your family—however goofy and irritating they may sometimes be—and remember that love unites you as one.

3

Ephesians 4:32
FORGIVING YOUR CRAZY FAMILY

Do you love your family and also feel like they're driving you crazy? Join the club!

Whether you live with one parent or two, your grandparents or other relatives, or siblings or cousins, it's likely that you experience conflict at home. Maybe that comes in the form of constant fighting with a stepparent, frustration at being misunderstood, or feeling awkward about sharing your feelings with your family.

When you spend time with someone, you discover their flaws and they uncover yours. Since we're all sinful people, our selfishness creeps out and stains our relationships. Small annoyances can fester and turn into screaming matches where doors are slammed and emotional walls are built up.

How do we handle this in a godly way?

First, recognize your sinful nature. We have to be honest and admit that we, too, have flaws and that we often contribute to problems. Just as we admit our mistakes to Jesus and receive His grace, we can talk to our family, apologize, and ask for forgiveness. Ephesians 4:32 reminds us,

*Be kind to one another, tenderhearted, forgiving
one another, as God in Christ forgave you.*

Next, we resolve to talk to the person we're struggling with instead of keeping our pain inside. It's unhealthy to let things fester, so take this step as quickly as you can. If you don't know what to say, try writing a letter to the family member you want to talk to. It may take a few drafts, but the act of writing your thoughts out will help clarify what you want to express.

Finally, remember that the Holy Spirit can change hearts, even if it seems like a broken relationship is beyond repair. Talk to Jesus about your problems, and trust that the Holy Spirit will be with you as you interact with your family. Remember that you have the chance to grow as you navigate all the good and bad situations of life, including wrestling through your conflict with the people in your household.

Thank God for the gift of family, who continue to love us despite the bumps in our relationships. Their love gives us a small glimpse of the endless love of Jesus, whose love for us led Him to suffer and die for us so that we would receive all the benefits as God's beloved children.

Faith Notes

....
....
....
....

4

Colossians 3:20

COMMUNICATING EFFECTIVELY WITH YOUR PARENTS

In all my years of ministering to young people, one of the most constant refrains I've heard is "I don't know how to tell my parents about this."

The prospect of sharing something difficult with our parents is intimidating. Even those of us with good relationships with our moms, dads, stepparents, and legal guardians can struggle to approach tough conversations with confidence. It's hard enough to admit that we've messed up, and it's even tougher to face the conversation knowing that they might react with anger, fear, or judgment.

Unfortunately, navigating these challenging conversations is a necessary skill for adulthood. You have to learn how to do it if you want to grow up to be a functional adult.

As Colossians 3:20 reminds us,

> Children, obey your parents in everything,
> for this pleases the Lord.

Obedience extends to having honest and respectful communication with your parents. Positive communication can build trust and allow your parents to better understand your struggles. In turn, they can provide guidance and support, helping you navigate your problems with wisdom.

Many girls are terrified to tell their parents something serious, and we often mentally exaggerate our parents' reaction to news. Here are a few things to try:

☐ Write your parents a letter to let them know what's going on. Practice a few drafts, if needed, until you can write the letter from a calm place of honesty. Don't blame or attack; just stick to the facts. End your letter by asking your parents to pray over what you've just confessed and then talk with you when they're ready to discuss it.

☐ Worried your parents might explode? Ask them to meet you for coffee or a smoothie. Sometimes a neutral site can help keep tempers (and reactions) in check.

☐ Share your situation with a Christian adult (a pastor, teacher, youth leader, grandparent, or coach) who can provide some perspective and wisdom in helping you tell your parents. Ask if they might be willing to meet with you and your parents together to help mediate the conversation.

☐ Text your parents something that expresses that you want to have a difficult conversation with them and that you need them to be in a calm headspace in order for you to open up. Ask them to let you know when it's a good time to talk.

☐ Role play the conversation with a trusted friend or adult in order to feel more confident and at ease in sharing your situation. Ask the other person to play your parent, while you be yourself.

As you navigate difficult conversations, remember that your parents love you fiercely. They may be disappointed or angry for a while, but nothing can change their love for you. Remember that your parents don't love you because you are good or obedient or pretty or smart. They love you because you are their very own precious child.

In the same way, nothing can change God's love for you! You are God's own precious child—the one Jesus sacrificed His life for. God's love wins out even over your worst mistakes. Let this knowledge of being accepted, loved, and forgiven by your heavenly Father give you the strength to be honest with your parents.

Faith Notes

....
....
....
....
....
....
....
....

5

Joshua 24:15

WHAT KIND OF FUTURE FAMILY WILL YOU HAVE?

M y family is so messed up," the high schooler sitting across from me said. "I don't want to end up divorced and screwing up my kids' lives and hating my life, like my parents."

Maybe you can relate to this sentiment about your own family situation. Perhaps it's messy—real messy—and you're worried that, somehow, you'll end up repeating the mistakes of your parents. Or perhaps the drama you've experienced in your family has made you bitter, jaded, and resentful. Maybe you've told yourself that you'll never trust anyone enough to have a serious relationship, let alone get married and have a family.

We cannot deny that many families are broken, and a lot of us have experienced significant pain and heartache as a result of these unfortunate circumstances. But your story doesn't have to be the same story as your parents, grandparents, or siblings. You can choose to live differently and make better choices.

The foundation you start to put in place today will shape your future—including your future family. And the firmest foundation anyone can have is Christ at the center of everything. In Joshua 24:15, Joshua says,

But as for me and my house, we will serve the LORD.

Why is Jesus so important as the foundation for your future family? Because it anchors your belief and confidence in His forgiveness, love, and unity. Making this a priority now becomes an important value that defines the rest of your life. When your faith in Jesus matters to you, it impacts your view of the future, including your potential spouse and the way you'll treat your future family.

Imagine yourself thirty years from now. What kind of a life do you want to be living? What values will you hope your spouse or kids embody? How do you want love, joy, and forgiveness to be a part of the way you interact with the people around you?

To make this dream a reality, start today by placing Jesus at the center of your life. Make Jesus, who covers you with His grace, peace, and promise of salvation, the main part of your story. Pray for guidance from the Holy Spirit as you grow and make decisions about who you want to be and what matters most to you. Spend regular time in prayer and worship, and practice sharing Jesus' love with the community around you.

With priorities like these set in place, you'll be creating a strong foundation for a future filled with love.

Journal about three things you want your future to include.

6

Galatians 6:2

SUPPORTING FAMILY IN TOUGH TIMES

One of my dear friends, Ryan, is a pastor. He's faithfully served others for his entire career, yet he has endured some really tough situations in his personal life. He fought for his first marriage only to have it end in divorce; then he married a wonderful woman who was diagnosed with breast cancer and passed away.

On his own, he raised his stepdaughter and daughter before he eventually met another great woman. They married and blended their families, so now Ryan has a big, happy family on his hands.

Ryan's journey hasn't been easy, but his family was an incredible source of support for him through every tough time. Every time Ryan and I talked as he was going through such painful struggles, he told me about how grateful he was for his family.

All families face difficult circumstances from time to time. It might mean weathering a financial change or job loss, divorce, serious illness or death, moving or changing schools and churches, or any number of other challenges.

God has blessed us with our families and intends for them to be a place of love and support, especially during trying times. We should make an extra effort to be there for our siblings, parents, and extended families when times are tough. As Galatians 6:2 says,

Bear one another's burdens, and so fulfill the law of Christ.

So what are some ways you can support your family members during tough times? One important thing you can do is pray with and for your family. You can also take the time to ask questions and listen with empathy. If the situation calls for it, you can offer to brainstorm and collaborate with your family members to find solutions to and new perspectives on problems. And you can always help with tasks around the house without being asked.

Don't forget to use your words to extend encouragement and hope too. Find ways to express your love through notes, conversations, and acts of service. Keep in mind that stressful situations may cause people to be on edge and easily frustrated. Make sure to offer understanding and forgiveness freely, just as Christ offers it to you.

Our families are all different and our paths through life are all different, yet both are important demonstrations of God's blessing and purpose for you. No matter what you and your family may face, trust that the triune God will continue to guide and support you every step of the way, through Jesus, who lived and died for you.

Journal about a time members of your family showed support for each other.

7

Proverbs 15:1

THE POWER OF SAYING YOU'RE SORRY

I'm sorry.
Two words that are so hard to say, right?

As we navigate life, frustrations and misunderstandings are bound to emerge in our relationships. Although we try to bite our tongues and control our behavior, sometimes harsh words and problematic decisions slip out. Whether we get caught lying or cheating or maybe outed for hurting someone, it's important to recognize when we've messed up and to own up to it.

Often, the people closest to us—usually, our family—bear the brunt of our bad behavior. After being on your best behavior all day, you might snap at your parents or siblings over something small. Unfortunately, that small spat can easily grow into a larger one, just like a snowball rolling downhill can become an avalanche.

Proverbs 15:1 reminds us,

> A soft answer turns away wrath, but
> a harsh word stirs up anger.

When we acknowledge how we've wronged someone and humbly ask for forgiveness, we emulate the love of Jesus.

More often than not, admitting we're wrong and asking for forgiveness also dissipates the problem.

When we recognize our moments of poor decision-making and acknowledge what we've done wrong, we grow in maturity and strength. Apologizing isn't an act of weakness; it's an act of courage—the courage to be real, admit you're not perfect, and seek to be better the next time.

When we say "I'm sorry" to people we've hurt, it can change their heart and ours. Even though it's hard to say (and maybe you think you had a good reason for acting the way you did in the first place), relationships are a gift from God that we need to protect and treasure.

Of course, Jesus is our example of compassion and humility. Even when He was beaten and cruelly nailed to the cross, He chose to obey God by giving His life for people—then and now. Not only did He forgive those who brutalized Him but He defeated the devil, overcame death, and won eternal life for us. When we remember all that Jesus did for us, we can be gracious to the people around us.

Spend some quiet time asking the Holy Spirit to bring to mind anyone who needs an apology from you. Maybe this person is a parent, sibling, or cousin you've hurt, and it's time to be brave in owning up to your mistakes and pursuing reconciliation. By being brave and apologizing, you have the chance to model the love of Christ and create a culture of grace in your life.

Activity

Who in your family tends to bear the burden of your angry outbursts? While we all make mistakes, it's not fair to let one person be your emotional punching bag. Pray about how you can grow and mature in this area, and consider how you can apologize and change your behavior in the future.

....
....
....
....
....
....
....
....
....
....
....
....
....
....
....
....
....
....

8

Romans 12:10
FAMILY FRUSTRATIONS

When we were growing up, my younger brother and I got along. Usually.

I remember a particular time when we were throwing rocks at each other, as goofy little kids without a fully developed prefrontal cortex do. We were both athletic, but my brother was a tennis ace and could whip rocks at me with stunning accuracy.

Our friendly competition at who could hurl rocks the farthest quickly turned hostile, and I ran off to tattle on him while dodging rocks that whistled around my head like grenades.

We laugh about it now, but I was sure mad at him at the time.

It doesn't matter if you have one sibling or parent or a whole passel of stepsiblings, brothers, sisters, and four parents and stepparents—family frustration is real and knows no bounds. Sometimes a younger sibling struggles to live in the shadow of the seemingly perfect older sister or brother. Other times, the middle child feels overlooked and left out. Older siblings can feel overwhelmed with the burden of responsibility and expectations. Adopted siblings and stepsiblings and stepparents can have a hard time figuring out how to fit in and find their place in the family.

It's natural to encounter bumps in your relationships with family members. We're all imperfect and trying to grow and mature, and that can lead to lots of friction. Even the closest families fight and become frustrated with each other. As Romans 12:10 reminds us,

> Love one another with brotherly affection.
> Outdo one another in showing honor.

Even when we get angry with our family members, we're called to be devoted to each other in the same love and grace Christ extends to us. When we embrace selflessness rather than competition, we can grow in our ability to appreciate the unique characters that make up our family. After all, these people will be a part of your life longer than anyone else! Our family's presence in our lives can remind us of who we are and where we came from, long into our twilight years. God intends for our families to be a source of support during tough times.

The next time you get frustrated with your siblings, parents, or stepparents, pause and remember the unique bond that you have. Remember that you'll likely be a part of each other's lives for a long time and that God has called you to love just as He loves you unconditionally in His Son, Jesus. Let your words and actions with your brothers and sisters reflect the love of Jesus that fills your soul.

9

John 13:34
LOVING UNCONDITIONALLY

L ife would be so much easier without other people, right? No, it wouldn't. But you know what I mean. Sometimes it feels like our friends and family just don't get us. Every once in a while, we're tempted to think that we shouldn't have to put up with them; they add too much stress, drama, and frustration to our lives.

If you've ever watched a ballroom dancing competition, have you noticed how the couples weave around each other? As the music plays, they spin, twist, and pull around each other. They're in the dance together but often move in different directions.

Life is a lot like ballroom dancing. Within our relationships, we twist around each other—together, but sometimes moving in different ways. The dance of relationships seems to be the most challenging when it comes to our families, where we choreograph respect, love, and discovery for each person into our rhythm. It's not easy, and we're bound to step on each other's toes. But without each other, the dance doesn't work.

Our family is a gift from God, and each person in it brings his or her own unique movement to the group.

Despite the hurt that they may cause us, our family members are a constant presence in our lives. We must learn how to dance with them, accepting their flaws and strengths just as they accept ours.

The art of navigating this complicated dance with our family may take a lifetime to master, but it's one we must attempt. Even when family lets us down or hurts us, they're still in our lives. We must learn to live with both their good and bad traits without becoming bitter or separating from them. John 13:34 reminds us,

A new commandment I give to you, that you love one another: just as I have loved you, you also are to love one another.

God calls us to live in the same love He extends to us, which is unconditional. This love isn't dependent on how others behave or whether they live up to our expectations. Rather, this unconditional love is from God, and it's sacrificial and selfless, given freely even when it is not deserved.

Even when someone we love hurts us, we can extend forgiveness and mercy to them just as Jesus does for us. This sort of love doesn't mean accepting harmful or hurtful behavior though. But if we have to put up protective boundaries, we can love and respect someone without mirroring their actions or choices.

When faced with challenges with the people in your life, let Christ's love be your guide. He loves us without reservation, and when we embrace this love, we can dance through life with joy and gratitude.

1

1 Samuel 16:7

EMBRACING GOD'S DEFINITION OF BEAUTY

If you could change one thing about yourself, what would it be?

Every girl I know can answer that question without thinking. We typically envision something we hate about our appearance. Whether you dislike your nose or thighs or wish you were skinnier, taller, or less freckled, it's easy to wish we looked different.

Our world is obsessed with appearances. Filters and photo editors abound, creating a whirlpool of negativity that can suck our self-confidence down the drain.

As you scroll through social media and YouTube, it can feel difficult to measure your life against the perfectly curated, retouched photos and videos we see from others.

I've felt pressure to conform to these beauty standards. I've plucked and primped, squeezed into painful shoes, and practiced poses to hide my insecurities from coming across in photos. I know I'm not alone in this either. From childhood on, this is the reality that women face in a world that is obsessed with unrealistic beauty standards.

Even when we say we don't care—let's be honest—a little bit of us still cares.

In contrast to what the world tells us we should look like, Scripture reminds us that true beauty wells up from within. As 1 Samuel 16:7 tells us,

> For the LORD sees not as man sees: man looks on the outward appearance, but the LORD looks on the heart.

Cut through the noise of societal pressures and embrace God's grace like a comforting sweatshirt you can snuggle into. He knows us, inside and out, and He doesn't mind if our hair is frizzy or our zits are on full display.

When the world bombards you with unrealistic standards, remind yourself that you're fearfully and wonderfully made in God's image. Remind your sisters in Christ to love themselves for who God created them to be and who Jesus redeemed them to be, rather than being obsessed with perfection that none of us can attain.

Living wrapped up in the peace of God's unconditional love, knowing that our souls are treasured, offers a comfort that outweighs everything else. His standard of beauty matters more than the ever-changing pressures of this world.

Faith Notes

....
....
....

2

1 Corinthians 13:4–8
TOXIC RELATIONSHIPS

I t's normal that he told me to lose some weight, right? That I need to spend a little more time at the gym?"

I reeled, shocked at what my high school student was recounting about a recent conversation with a guy she liked. Addison was beautiful and athletic and definitely didn't need to lose weight. I couldn't believe a guy was filling her head with nonsense that was hurting her self-confidence.

Over a long chat at a coffee shop, she eventually recognized that her relationship with this boy was toxic.

You wouldn't believe how many girls I counsel through harmful relationships. Usually these relationships involve a guy or a friend who displays controlling behavior, betrays and lies, and destroys trust. Sometimes, though, it's a family member who causes massive issues.

When you're in a toxic relationship, it seems like you may never be happy again. You're often walking on eggshells around someone, and you're made to feel like everything you do is wrong and that everything about you is unacceptable. Perhaps you've even become isolated and have pulled away from the people who genuinely love you and the things you enjoy.

How do you know when a relationship might be toxic? Simply put, if a relationship never brings joy and instead causes you pain, you may be trapped in a toxic situation. Other clues include you experiencing emotions of anger, anxiety, sadness, insecurity, or resignation over and over. Perhaps you feel irritation or envy when you look at healthy relationships, or maybe your self-esteem or mental health has taken a hit.

If you find yourself checking these boxes, open up to someone you trust. Sharing the truth of your toxic relationship with a wise family member, teacher, coach, pastor, or youth leader is an important step for you to start to untangle from something unhealthy.

God puts caring people in our path because we aren't intended to do life alone. Ask the Holy Spirit to show you who you can go to for help in these difficult situations. And if you're not in a toxic relationship yourself, perhaps someone you know is and needs help.

The words of 1 Corinthians 13:4–8 paint a picture of the healthy love that God offers to us:

Love is patient and kind; love does not envy or boast; it is not arrogant or rude. It does not insist on its own way; it is not irritable or resentful; it does not rejoice at wrongdoing, but rejoices with the truth. Love bears all things, believes all things, hopes all things, endures all things. Love never ends.

Allow this truth to permeate your life. The love this passage describes is from Jesus, and it comes to us unconditionally—that is, without our having to behave a certain way or look a certain way or say the right things. Everything we know about how Jesus loves us is written in the Bible for us to learn and take to heart. Embrace this truth through reading the Bible, praying and worshiping, and receiving love through fellow believers. As you grapple with the challenges of earthly relationships, never forget that God's love for you is perfect and unending.

Faith Notes

....

....

....

....

....

....

....

....

....

....

....

....

....

....

3

Psalm 139:13–14

RESISTING PRESSURE FROM OTHERS

One of the worst feelings in the world is not being accepted.

Girls can be especially cruel at excluding each other. We find reasons to push others out and keep our circles small. Friendships often change as drama escalates. We create imaginary rules about maintaining our status at the expense of including other people.

The challenges of peer pressure have existed since the beginning of time, and they certainly haven't lessened with each new generation that emerges. Girls often pressure one another to adopt certain body images, trends, clothes, or makeup. Sometimes we pressure each other into relationships, risky behavior, or trying something forbidden.

When I was in high school, a girl on my soccer team was inundated with pressure from her best friend to lose weight. I remember her friend teasing her in the locker room every day, pinching her stomach and telling her she was fat. Within a year, my teammate had developed an eating disorder and had to be hospitalized for an extended stay in order to save her life.

The desire to fit in can destroy us. So what can we do to resist negative peer pressure?

First of all, it's important to recognize your worth. You're more than a face, a body, an athlete, a scholar, or a girlfriend. You are valuable, an individual created special by our almighty God. He gives you purpose and an identity as a baptized and redeemed child of the King.

Second, work to understand your personal values. When you are certain of what matters to you, it's easier to resist pressure that contradicts those values. What matters most to you? What people do you admire and want to be like? What qualities do you care about? How do you want to live your life? What are the lines you will not cross?

Third, look for genuine friends who love you for who you are. Real friends will encourage you and speak truth rather than push you to conform. Having authentic people in your life can build your self-confidence and remind you that you are God's precious child. Don't be afraid to connect with trusted adults for their guidance and advice as you navigate this road.

Psalm 139:13–14 remind us that we are created by God as unique individuals:

> For You formed my inward parts; You knitted me together in my mother's womb. I praise You, for I am fearfully and wonderfully made. Wonderful are Your works; my soul knows it very well.

In Christ, you are fully accepted for who you are: a beautiful young woman who was handmade by God and designed for His purpose, which is to give Him honor and glory and to serve Him where He has you right now.

You are just what God created you to be, and He delights in you.

Faith Notes

....
....
....
....
....
....
....
....
....
....
....
....
....
....
....
....
....
....
....
....

4

Psalm 139:23–24
KNOW THYSELF

H ow well do you know yourself?

The famous Greek maxim to "know thyself" is an important parcel of wisdom to possess, especially when it comes to relationships. Without the self-awareness that comes from understanding how you're wired, you can unintentionally sabotage relationships, hurt others, and even compromise your values in dating, friendships, and future opportunities.

Psalm 139:23–24 gives us words to offer up to God:

Search me, O God, and know my heart! Try me and know my thoughts! And see if there be any grievous way in me, and lead me in the way everlasting!

Knowing yourself begins with spending some time understanding your character, values, and boundaries. When you honestly assess your strengths and weaknesses, inviting the Holy Spirit to reveal blind spots and growth areas through God's Word, prayer, and the people God has placed around you, you can better discern who you really are.

When you know who you are, you're better equipped to communicate your needs and boundaries to others. This is the foundation for healthy relationships. It gives you the confidence to speak up and say no when you're uncomfortable and yes when it's appropriate.

Young women often struggle with boundaries in relationships, especially with guys. By knowing who you are—God's precious creation—you can communicate your standards and expectations with quiet confidence.

Don't ever let someone else push you to do something you're not comfortable with. By figuring out what standards you have for yourself, you can set clear expectations well in advance of any pressure-filled, emotional situations.

Trust that God knows your heart and ask Him to give you the wisdom to navigate the path forward in a safe and productive way. Pray for continued insight into knowing yourself so you can keep building more fulfilling connections that are anchored in faith and self-awareness. And have confidence in Jesus, who gave His very life for you, to love you and forgive you.

Faith Notes

....
....
....
....
....
....

5

Proverbs 4:23
BOUNDARIES

One of the nicest dates I ever went on was with a guy who took me to an art museum. As we wandered through the huge galleries, staring at the massive oil paintings, I dropped all sorts of art history knowledge on him.

"I'm impressed," he finally said, strolling next to me. "You should be a tour guide! You know way more than I even thought you did about art!"

I sure did. Because I'd been to the museum with my collegiate art class just a few days before.

I had decided not to tell him that in an effort to appear more knowledgeable than I really was.

We've all experienced the pressure to prove ourselves and project an image of experience beyond what we possess. The pressure to seem like you've got it all together is a big one, and it hits us from all corners of relationships. This can push us to compromise our values or pretend to be someone we're not in an attempt to fit in or earn approval.

The reality, though, is that being authentic and vulnerable is far more important than trying to live up to unrealistic expectations. We can bear false witness about ourselves as well as about others. Proverbs 4:23 tells us,

> Keep your heart with all vigilance, for
> from it flow the springs of life.

This verse is important as we consider the boundaries we create for ourselves. We must guard our hearts instead of giving in to pressure from others and from our own sinful state. Healthy, Jesus-centered relationships allow you to be your genuine self without making you pretend or prove something. The first step toward that is being honest with Jesus. We can confess everything, big and little, being completely transparent with the One who forgives our sins. Jesus understands us and loves us anyway. Jesus was true to who He was (the Son of God) and what He was sent to do (take away our sins). Now we can be true to who we are (daughters of God) and do what we are created to do (give glory to God and serve others).

You know that God has blessed you with a good relationship when someone loves you for who you are, quirks and shortcomings and all. Guarding your heart means making good relationships a priority rather than trying to impress people who won't accept you unless you pretend.

Trust that God will bring the right people into your life to bring you encouragement and joy. Seek your worth from being a child of God rather than seeking empty validation from others.

6

Isaiah 41:10
DON'T HESITATE; GET HELP

The concert had just started when one of my students jumped out of her seat and sprinted for the exit.

I followed and discovered that she was experiencing a full-fledged panic attack. We ducked into the back of the stadium as she sobbed, hyperventilated, and swayed with dizziness.

If you've never had a panic attack, count your blessings. It's a terrifying episode of intense anxiety. Your mind and body veer out of control, and you can experience shortness of breath, lightheadedness, a racing heart, and muscle tension. Sometimes a scary situation can prompt a panic attack. Other times, accumulated stress can put you on edge and elicit feelings of overwhelming fear and worry. In these moments of anxiety, it may feel like the world is closing in. You may feel alone, like no one could possibly understand what you're going through.

God assures us that we are not alone in these worrisome situations. Isaiah 41:10 reminds us,

> Fear not, for I am with you; be not dismayed, for I am your God; I will strengthen you, I will help you, I will uphold you with My righteous right hand.

I led my student through breathing activities to reset her mind and body, and she eventually calmed down.

"Thank you for not judging me for this," she replied, wiping away tears. "That makes all the difference."

In the same way, our Savior never judges us for the moments of weakness and brokenness we experience. He stays by our side, offering His strength and hope and keeping His promises of mercy and forgiveness. God has compassion on us, loves us, draws us close to Himself, and gives us refuge.

One of the ways God provides for us is by equipping people to help—people like counselors, medical doctors, psychiatrists, hospital chaplains, and emergency personnel. In some cases, a doctor will prescribe medication to help with symptoms.

If you or someone you know is having a debilitating anxiety attack, seek help immediately. Don't hesitate to ask for help.

For moments of everyday anxiety that can be managed, consider using coping techniques. Research shows that there are many helpful ways to deal with everyday anxiety, such as mindfulness, hugs, and journaling. As in everything, prayer and meditation on Scripture are valuable tools to use when anxious thoughts occur.

Let God's promises sink in and give you peace in those moments when you're panicked. With Him, you are never alone.

And that makes all the difference. Write a verse reminds you of His promises in your journal.

7

Song of Solomon 8:4; Galatians 6:1–2
TO BE LOVED

L ove is complicated. And naturally, it's something we try to analyze because it's such a tricky subject with far-reaching implications for our lives. It's the favorite subject of songs, books, and sleepovers for good reason: it impacts all of us.

It's natural to want to give and receive love. When love is exchanged in healthy relationships, there's no sense of shame or regret. Yet so many of us experience unhealthy forms of love, from what we see online and in the media to what we experience from others.

Song of Solomon 8:4 advises,

> [Do] not stir up or awaken love until it pleases.

This verse indicates the importance of holding to boundaries that line up with Scripture. Respecting yourself and God means that you stay true to the values and expectations He has put in place for all of us.

However, even good people can push our boundaries too far. While intimacy is a beautiful thing, God puts clear limits on when and how it should occur. If someone is pressuring you beyond what you're comfortable with, it's critical that you have the courage to speak up and tell them about your boundaries. Even if you can't stand to hurt someone else, to stifle your own feelings and let yourself be put in a difficult situation will only cause you pain and regret. And think of this—allowing someone else to behave in harmful ways that are not in alignment with what the Bible tells us is allowing that person to sin. It's our responsibility as followers of Jesus to gently but firmly point out their wrong behavior.

> Brothers, if anyone is caught in any transgression, you who are spiritual should restore him in a spirit of gentleness. Keep watch on yourself, lest you too be tempted. Bear one another's burdens, and so fulfill the law of Christ. (Galatians 6:1–2)

I can't tell you how many times a student has called me in tears, regretting what they've done. They often feel deep shame and embarrassment, and sometimes the resulting circumstances can have life-altering implications.

When you make mistakes of your own or blow past your boundaries, cling to the comfort of God's forgiveness. Even in your lowest moments of regret and humiliation, God's grace is offered freely. No mistake is too big for God's mercy. Remember Jesus' parable of the prodigal son? Jesus welcomes you with unconditional love, abundant forgiveness, and enduring joy. And that's a promise.

No matter what situation you may find yourself in, God is never done with you. Your life will continue to be filled with plenty of blessings. Because of His boundless love, we have hope.

Embrace God's grace, earned for you by Jesus' sacrifice on the cross, as you learn from your mistakes and gain the confidence to hold firm to your boundaries.

Faith Notes

....
....
....
....
....
....
....
....
....
....
....
....
....
....
....
....
....
....
....
....

1

Colossians 3:12–14
WHAT ARE YOUR VALUES?

Have you ever been lost and had to rely on a compass to navigate to your destination?

In life, our values act as a compass to guide our decisions and shape who we become. It's an important part of growing up to spend some time discerning who you are, how you choose to live, and what values define both of those things.

To discover your personal values, start by listing how you aspire to live. What matters to you? Some common values are honesty, humility, perseverance, and compassion. As you think about what you want to embody, weigh these values against Scripture. Do they align with God's commands? Do they match the traits you see in Jesus?

Colossians 3:12–14 serves as a great reminder of the values that God desires for us to embody as His children:

> Put on then, as God's chosen ones, holy and beloved, compassionate hearts, kindness, humility, meekness, and patience, bearing with one another and, if one has a complaint against another, forgiving each other; as the Lord has forgiven you, so you also

must forgive. And above all these put on love, which
binds everything together in perfect harmony.

After you list several values, underline the top two or
three that resonate most with you. Is there a common
theme among them? What new insights do these unlock
about what matters in your life?

Spend some time looking at the lives of the people
who inspire you, whether those are public role models or
faithful adults you know. What values do they display?
Think about if you want to add any of these values to
your own list.

If you're struggling to figure out your values, try
identifying the values you want to avoid. Maybe you'll
realize that you hate when people are fake so you value
authenticity or that your dislike of greed indicates that
you value generosity.

As you discern your values and start to prioritize
them in your life, you'll find purpose in your journey.
Your values will help guide you on the path that God
has designed for you. Continue growing and adding
new values to your list, knowing that Jesus serves as
the ultimate guide toward a life that reflects His grace
and love.

Faith Notes

....
....
....

2

1 Peter 4:11; Jeremiah 17:7

CREATING A MISSION STATEMENT

God gives us opportunities throughout our lives to discover who He has created us to be. One way to reflect on your identity is through writing a personal mission statement. This can help you uncover your God-given gifts, talents, values, and purpose.

So how do you create a personal mission statement? Start by spending some quiet time thinking about what brings you happiness, what you're good at, and what gives your life meaning. List these things, then fill in the blanks of the sentence below:

"I value

_____

(*your most important values*),
and I want to use my God-given ability of

_____

(*your spiritual gifts and skills*) to

_____

(*something that brings you meaning*)."

If you start to feel overwhelmed by trying to narrow this down to a single sentence, remember that your mission statement isn't set in stone forever—it's just a snapshot of you at this moment. Just as you grow and change, your mission statement may change. Embrace this growth, knowing that your journey is part of God's plan and that He will continue to equip you.

Sometimes we're tempted to undercut ourselves and dismiss how God may use us. We may tell ourselves that we're too messed up, too shy, too unfocused, or too awkward to be used as a vessel of the Holy Spirit.

But God used imperfect people throughout the Bible to accomplish His purposes—despite their shortcomings! Think of Moses, Rahab, David, Zacchaeus, and Paul. Their lives were full of missteps and mistakes, yet God's grace transformed their lives for His greater purpose.

In 1 Peter 4:11, we are given a clear reminder that our purpose is grounded in glorifying God:

> Whoever speaks, as one who speaks oracles of God; whoever serves, as one who serves by the strength that God supplies—in order that in everything God may be glorified through Jesus Christ. To Him belong glory and dominion forever and ever. Amen.

God's love is unwavering, even if we don't know exactly where we're going or what we're doing. We can trust that our Creator made us beautifully complex and that He will use us to accomplish His will. And we can go forward in confidence that we are secure in Him.

Blessed is the man who trusts in the LORD,
whose trust is the LORD. (Jeremiah 17:7)

Let this truth be a comfort as you navigate life's journey.

Activity

Engage in the exercise on the previous pages and write out a mission statement. It may take a few drafts to come up with something concise—that's okay! When you're done, share it with trustworthy friends or adults. Ask for them to give some feedback and listen to what they may share. Perhaps they see something in you that you don't see. Jot down what you learn from their response, and prayerfully consider if the Holy Spirit might be using them to bring new insight to you.

....
....
....
....
....
....
....
....
....
....
....
....
....

3

Matthew 16:26
BUILDING YOUR REPUTATION

O ver the past year, I've become friends with an older woman, Linda, who sleeps outside of my office. Linda is homeless.

And when I say that we've become friends, I mean it. We know all about each other's lives, families, pets, and problems. In fact, we talk almost every day as I leave the office and head home from work.

Recently, Linda and I talked about how people treat her. "Sometimes people pull up to me and offer me food or money," she said. "Other times, they roll down their car window and scream and swear at me, calling me lazy and stupid."

Despite what people assume of Linda as they drive by, her reputation is well known in our community. She considers herself a street chaplain, and I've seen her helping other homeless people get groceries and medical care. She prays for others—including me—and reads her Bible every day. Linda helps others all the time.

You see, reputation isn't something you can simply create. It's a reflection of your actions, behaviors, character, and choices. You earn a reputation based on the way you interact with others and the value-shaped decisions you make. Every day, your words and choices will influence how others perceive you.

Although your reputation is built one choice at a time, it's also possible to tear it down one choice at a time. Perhaps you're struggling with the effects of sending that photo or going to that party or dating that person or using that language. Remember that God's grace is bigger than any failure of yours. His forgiveness offers you a fresh start. In time, relationships can be mended, mistakes can fade into the background, and reputations can be rebuilt.

In Matthew 16:26, Jesus tells us that gaining worldly success means nothing if it costs us our souls:

> For what will it profit a man if he gains the whole world and forfeits his soul? Or what shall a man give in return for his soul?

To God, the most important goal in life is living in a way that honors Him and brings His love and grace to other people. As you go through life, make choices that are consistent with the person God created you to be. Embrace compassion, love, and humility and see how these values impact your reputation. And even when you blow it, you can take solace in the knowledge that God sees the depth of your heart, knows the extent of your mistakes, and sent Jesus to save you from your sins anyway. He loves you unconditionally.

Activity

Using paper and markers, build a Good Reputation Box.
You can bend, fold, or cut the paper into any shape to
make this box. Write qualities on the sides of the box
that describe a person with a good reputation.

As you look over the box, consider how tricky it was to construct
it with no instructions. This is a metaphor for life: there are no
easy directions! It's a process of trial and error, and it takes time.

Remember that our reputation is built one day at a time
by the choices we make. Spend a few minutes praying
about where on your box you need to embrace the grace
to grow. Cover up this spot on your box with a post-it note
that says, "God's grace is bigger than my failure."

....
....
....
....
....
....
....
....
....
....
....
....

4

Luke 10:27–28
GOAL GETTER

When I was ten, I had an ambitious goal: I wanted to publish a book by the time I was thirty. Fast-forward two decades, and my first book was published when I was twenty-nine.

Even at a young age, I knew that I wanted my words to bring joy and connection to people I didn't know. As an author, nothing makes me happier than meeting someone who has read something I wrote and who tells me that my words helped bring comfort or insight.

Some of us have strong goals from a young age, and we set out to tackle them with single-minded focus. I have good friends who are doctors, lawyers, homeschool moms, and veterinarians, and many of them realized their passion when they were little and set goals to direct their path toward accomplishing their dreams.

Others, though, take a while to discern what they want to accomplish. I think of these people as "taste-testers" of life: they sample a lot of things in order to figure out what they like. Many of my friends who have creative careers, like graphic design, entrepreneurship, and nonprofit leadership, followed paths filled with twists and turns on their way to their current positions.

Whatever your path may be and however you might be wired, trust that God has an important purpose for your life. Maybe the unique gift you share with the world is an ability to make others laugh. Or maybe you're someone who helps others feel less alone in their struggles.

However you bless the world around you, know that your life matters. The unique gifts God has given you can be used for His glory in ways you may not even recognize until you look back when you are older.

Whatever our goals may be, they should be in step with what God desires for His children to pursue. In Luke 10:27–28, Jesus shared an important reminder of where our focus should be:

> And [the lawyer] answered, "You shall love the Lord your God with all your heart and with all your soul and with all your strength and with all your mind, and your neighbor as yourself." And [Jesus] said to him, "You have answered correctly; do this, and you will live."

Our lives should reflect a pursuit of giving glory to God and sharing His redemptive love with the people around us.

Having goals about your future is helpful as you navigate these years of personal growth. A goal is simply your aim: a result toward that which your effort is directed. Your goal can be personal ("I want to learn to play guitar") or it can be oriented toward blessing someone else ("I want to bring encouragement to others by writing cheerful notes every day").

One of the best ways to set goals is to think about what you enjoy doing and what talents God has blessed you with. Perhaps there's a goal hidden within a joy that you can use to serve God and positively impact the world.

Your goals are best when they're challenging but realistic. Ideally, they're set just beyond your reach but not so far out of reach that you have no hope of achieving them. As the adage says, "Shoot for the moon, and even if you miss, you'll land among the stars." Don't forget to write them down, as research shows that we recall and accomplish our goals better when we put pen to paper.

As you reflect on your goals, check your instincts. Our culture is me-focused, which tempts us to create a list of self-centered goals. Honestly evaluate your goals and consider if they are in line with the life God designed you for and if they are strengthening your walk with Jesus.

Thinking about the future can be exciting and nerve-racking at the same time. But take comfort in knowing that God created you with purpose, sent His Son to forgive your sin and restore you to God, and will patiently guide you to exactly where you need to be at every crossroads in your life. Your future is in good hands.

Faith Notes

....
....

5

1 Timothy 4:12; Proverbs 18:21; Ephesians 4:15
COMMUNICATE CLEARLY

I recently spent a weekend with friends, hanging out at a beach house together to celebrate my goddaughter's Baptism. As we sat around one evening, I helped Kensley, one of my goddaughters, make a bracelet.

Her tiny fingers carefully picked up each plastic bead, examining and rejecting multiple options before settling on a giant blue gem. She strung it on the cord, concentration evident in her face, before selecting another bead.

I watched as she picked up a blue gem just like the one she'd just put on and started to string it.

"Kensley, don't you want another color?" I suggested, holding up another bead. "You just did a blue one!"

"No," she replied, looking up at me. "I like blue."

"But here's a pretty pink one," I said, holding it out to her.

"No," she repeated, fixing me with a steely gaze. "Blue."

I smiled as I watched her put the identical bead on. It turned out she was making the bracelet for me, and it sits on my desk in a place of honor. It reminds me of the importance of being true to yourself and making your choices with confidence, even if they aren't what someone else might choose.

The world doesn't always appreciate when women speak their minds and make their own choices, but it's an essential part of your character development. The most admirable women I know have learned to set boundaries, speak their minds with honesty and tact, and be confident in who God has made them to be. As Paul wrote in 1 Timothy 4:12,

> Let no one despise you for your youth, but set the believers an example in speech, in conduct, in love, in faith, in purity.

Communicating clearly is a gift to ourselves and others. As followers of Jesus, our words can bring love and hope to the people around us. As Proverbs 18:21 reminds us,

> Death and life are in the power of the tongue,
> and those who love it will eat its fruits.

God gave you the gift of a unique voice, and He wants you to use it with purpose. When you speak up for truth, encourage others, and share messages of honesty and grace, you can positively impact the world for Christ by speaking words that are consistent with Scripture.

What does it look like to communicate clearly as a Christian? It means speaking up for yourself and others when something is wrong. It's having the tough conversation with a spirit of forgiveness and compassion. It's defending someone who is being mocked online or in whispers. It's sharing the truth rather than ghosting someone. It's being authentic in sharing how Jesus has helped you through your own struggles rather than keeping your testimony private.

> Rather, speaking the truth in love, we are to grow up in every way into Him who is the head, into Christ. (Ephesians 4:15)

Jesus is our light and salvation. Without Him as our Lord, everything falls apart. As you continue to grow, ask God for the wisdom to communicate with words that uplift rather than tear down. Look to Jesus as an example of how to share messages of truth in ways that bring understanding, compassion, and healing to others.

Your tongue has the power of life and death, so use it carefully. Remember that your words can impact hearts, minds, and souls. Speak with clarity and confidence, allowing your voice to be one that God uses to share His grace with the world.

Activity

Reflect on what your voice tends to say to others. Do you uplift and point out the good, or do you complain and focus on the negative? Do your words contain more joy or more criticism? Do you speak with compassion and tact, or are your words angry and hurtful? Write down two or three words that describe how you communicate right now, and draw an arrow to a positive trait you'd like to work on. Ask that God helps you to grow in this area and surrounds you with people who can model it for you.

6

Psalm 139:16; Luke 12:6–7

VALUED, NOT OVERLOOKED

I was standing outside my college dorm during a fire drill when I spotted a new face in the crowd. *I'll be friendly and introduce myself to her,* I told myself, walking over to greet this new student. *It must be her first week, and she probably doesn't know anyone.*

I reached her and extended my hand. "Nice to meet you," I smiled. "Are you new to campus?"

The girl stared at me with confusion and her eyes quickly narrowed. "Is this a joke? I've lived in your hall all year. We've met before. Am I that easy to forget?"

Well, I think we know the answer to that.

I was mortified. We had lived just a few rooms away from each other for months, and I'd completely overlooked her.

Can you relate to being overlooked?

Maybe you don't get the best grades or aren't the star on the team. Perhaps you're the one who doesn't say much or isn't really noticed. Perhaps this makes you feel unappreciated or unwanted. Maybe it affects the way you think about yourself or the way you think others feel about you.

Being a teenager means battling through feelings of being unnoticed and overlooked.

Your value comes from God, not from how others see you. You see, God is your Creator. He designed you with care and purpose, and He knows your value.

Scripture tells us that God adores us and that nothing escapes His attention. He knew us before we were born and knows exactly what's ahead for us. As Psalm 139:16 reminds us,

> Your eyes saw my unformed substance; in Your book were written, every one of them, the days that were formed for me, when as yet there was none of them.

Despite what others may overlook, God sees what is special in you, and He loves you fiercely with a love that will never fail.

Your worth doesn't come from standing out, performing well, or being noticed by the right person. Your worth comes from being His beloved child, crafted with unique gifts and a story all your own, and saved for all eternity by Jesus' love for you and life for you.

> Are not five sparrows sold for two pennies? And not one of them is forgotten before God. Why, even the hairs of your head are all numbered. Fear not; you are of more value than many sparrows. (Luke 12:6–7)

You are valued, not overlooked, by your heavenly Father. In your journal, thank God for His promise to always see and love you.

7

Ephesians 4:32; Colossians 3:12

HOW DO YOU TREAT OTHERS?

History is filled with stories of how one person's compassion can influence the world for the better. One such story is that of Oskar Schindler, a German businessman who ended up saving the lives of more than 1,200 Jewish people in Poland during World War II.

Schindler, initially a member of the Nazi Party, tried to profit from the war and saw firsthand how the Jewish people were being mistreated. Determined to do something to stop the evil he was witnessing, he used his factories as a front to employ Jewish workers to keep them from being deported to concentration camps. Schindler's courage was immortalized in a book and later, a movie, *Schindler's List*, which became an Academy Award–winning film. Although Schindler himself was far from perfect, his story reminds us that a person's willingness to stand up for others can make a big difference.

While you might not have the ability to save people's lives in such a dramatic manner, you nevertheless have many opportunities to treat others with compassion and thus share the love of Christ. Ephesians 4:32 tells us to

> Be kind to one another, tenderhearted, forgiving
> one another, as God in Christ forgave you.

Treating others with kindness, compassion, and patience serves as a contrast to the competitive, self-focused world we occupy. When you think about how your words or actions might affect others, choosing to speak well of them and treating them with benevolence, you pass on the acceptance and love that Christ has for you.

Our true character is revealed in small moments when we think no one is looking. What is truly in our hearts comes across in the anonymous comments we make online, the way we treat waiters and baristas and other drivers, and the manner in which we talk about others when we're not trying to impress someone.

So . . . how do you treat others? Are you thoughtful? a good listener? an encourager? Do you stand up for others? reject gossip? speak up for and defend those who are being bullied or mocked? refrain from snarky comments online? avoid sharing hurtful videos and jokes?

Or do you have some growth to do?

The wonderful thing about being part of God's family is that He knows where we struggle, and He gives us chance after chance to grow and change for the better. Even when we fail to be who God wants us to be, He meets our failure with grace and mercy in the form of His Son, Jesus.

Put on then, as God's chosen ones, holy and beloved, compassionate hearts, kindness, humility, meekness, and patience. (Colossians 3:12)

We can treat others with the same love we receive from Jesus, trusting that He uses us to make an impact in ways we may never see, drawing others closer to Him.

Faith Notes

....
....
....
....
....
....
....
....
....
....
....
....
....
....
....
....
....
....

8

Philippians 2:3
SELF-OBSESSED

I once had lunch with a friend who couldn't stop talking about herself. Her mouth moved a mile a minute, telling me about her job, the new outfits she'd bought, the purse she was saving up for, and how she was thinking about cutting her hair.

She was too busy talking about herself to notice, but I was picking at my food. My beloved grandpa had recently passed away, and I was still struggling with his sudden death.

When my friend finally noticed that my behavior was off, she put down her fork. "Are you okay?" she asked, concern on her face.

"Not really," I admitted, explaining how I was lost in grief. I was about to share more, but my friend interrupted me before I could get in another word.

"Oh, that stinks . . . but at least you don't have to deal with my problems," she blurted, launching afresh into another complaint.

Sometimes we're self-obsessed without even knowing it. Selfishness is a part of the condition of sin, and we're all guilty of thinking of ourselves first. Whether we take the cookie with the most chocolate chips or obsessively preen over appearance, grades, or social status instead of paying attention to a friend or holding up our end of the chores at home, our selfish nature rears its ugly head often.

Young women are hit hard by selfishness, as it's not just part of our sinful human nature but it's also a hallmark of adolescence development. As your body and brain continue to mature through the teenage years, your brain is hardwired to focus intently on you.

That's why it never used to bother you to walk into the room and have everyone turn to look at you, but suddenly it makes you super self-conscious. And that's why you freak about every freckle and pimple. When your brain is busy worrying about you, it doesn't have the capacity to think about others.

On top of this, selfishness is reinforced by the world around us. Think about how many advertisements tempt you to indulge and treat yourself, how many pictures people post of themselves being pampered and buying things or engaging in new experiences.

When we obsess about ourselves, the people around us get shifted to the back seat. Unfortunately, when someone is always stuck in the back seat, ignored and undervalued, they tend to climb out of the vehicle and look for someone else to ride alongside.

In contrast to all of this, God makes it clear that we are not to live as self-obsessed people. Philippians 2:3 reminds us,

> Do nothing from selfish ambition or conceit, but in humility count others more significant than yourselves.

As God's beloved and redeemed daughters, we can trust that we have been given everything we need. He is the source of our identity and through our Baptism has made us loved and valued members of His family. He is the source of our bodies and souls, minds and hearts, and He cares for each part of us. So, of course, He is the source of our future—the One who saved us with His sacrifice and promises us the gift of eternal life.

The next time you're tempted to think *me, me, me*, turn that selfish, self-obsessed behavior over to God. Remember that He has blessed you richly and that you have the opportunity to multiply those blessings by caring about the people around you.

It's not all about you—it's about what God has done for you.

Faith Notes

....
....
....
....
....
....
....

1

Proverbs 10:12; Matthew 5:43–45; John 1:16–17

TROLL TROUBLE

I bit my lip as I stared at the comment an anonymous troll had posted on my photo:

"You're ugly," it proclaimed. "You're nothing special at all."

I'd like to tell you that I easily brushed off this insult that someone had left in response to one of my published articles. But this happened more than a decade ago, and I can still remember every word of the venom, so I'd be lying if I told you it didn't still hurt.

In our increasingly digital world, learning to deal with online trolls is a necessary skill. While it's safe to assume that some bots are computer generated and not real people, a troll is a person who is intentionally cruel, offensive, provocative, or inflammatory. The people who hide behind anonymous accounts to attack, destroy, and discourage others are misguided—but they are still fellow human beings who deserve fair treatment.

It's important that we never forget that there are real people behind anonymous accounts and that we must respond with grace and compassion. Our witness to the world, as Christians, extends to our online profiles. Proverbs 10:12 advises,

> Hatred stirs up strife, but love covers all offenses.

When you're faced with ugliness from trolls, resist the desire to retaliate with anger. Instead, respond with an open heart. As Jesus instructed in Matthew 5:43–45,

> You have heard that it was said, "You shall love your neighbor and hate your enemy." But I say to you, Love your enemies and pray for those who persecute you, so that you may be sons of your Father who is in heaven. For He makes His sun rise on the evil and on the good, and sends rain on the just and on the unjust.

I once had a middle school student confess to me that he was an online troll, going after others on a gaming site. "Why do you do it?" I asked him, curious.

He thought for a moment. "I just really hate my life right now," he sighed. "I suppose it distracts me from how bad things are at home."

Unfortunately, trolls are often privately struggling. People usually don't make a habit of going after others unless they're terribly unhappy or have anger issues. As you deal with negativity online, remember that trolls may be seeking attention or a reaction to distract themselves from their own pain. When you politely refuse to engage, you deprive them of what they crave and give them an opportunity to take a step back and reset.

To protect yourself from hateful posts and to guard yourself from your own angry thoughts and words, be mindful of the Fifth Commandment to not murder—which includes anger and contempt. Remember to make good use of the privacy settings that social media has in place and block trolls from seeing your accounts online. And take the issue to God in prayer. Remember that Jesus came to uphold God's Law and also to accomplish it—by His birth, life, death, and resurrection—for us and even for trolls.

> For from His fullness we have all received, grace upon grace. For the law was given through Moses; grace and truth came through Jesus Christ. (John 1:16–17)

Don't forget that your worth isn't based on the negative words of others but on the identity that Christ gives you as His precious, redeemed creation. Surround yourself with encouraging people, online and in person, who remind you of this truth. Keep your eyes on Jesus and let His love guide your responses to trolls in your life.

Faith Notes

....
....
....
....
....

2

2 Corinthians 12:9
BEING REAL

I still chuckle when I think about the photo my friend Nick posted online a few years ago.

It was Easter weekend, and every picture I saw contained images of beaming families, dressed in beautiful clothes, faces perfectly lit, and the house or yard behind them immaculate.

In contrast, Nick's photo was a picture of his wife and him attempting to wrangle their three little girls. The kids were clearly fighting and sobbing, their Easter dresses rumpled and exasperated expressions on the faces of both parents. When I asked about it, Nick laughed. "That was the reality of what my Easter morning was like!"

Nick's honesty in sharing the genuine truth behind his Easter morning experience was refreshing. Far too many of us are afraid to let our real selves show, so we hide behind filters and flattering camera angles and cropped images. We're tempted to display perfection online rather than leaning into authenticity.

Yet our imperfections are all too real. We have zits and cellulite, tummy rolls and stains on our shirts, gaps in our teeth and weird expressions when we're caught laughing too hard. These are the little things that remind us that to be human is to be flawed. As 2 Corinthians 12:9 states,

My grace is sufficient for you, for My power is made perfect in weakness.

Our desire to hide is a result of original sin. Just like Adam and Eve tried to cover their disobedience, we try to cover our flaws. This effort puts up a barrier.

In my experience, people have always connected with me on a deeper level when I've been authentic. When you live vulnerably, God's mercy for us can shine through your brokenness. When we confess our imperfections, we allow God's love to work through our weaknesses and fill the cracks of our failures with His grace, forgiveness, and healing. God promised Adam and Eve that He would provide them with a solution to their sin, and He fulfilled that promise when Jesus paid the price for sin.

The next time you're tempted to tweak a photo and change the way you look in it, pause for a moment and remember that God loves you just as you are—quirks and all. His love is genuine, and it frees you to be genuinely you in a world of unrealistic standards.

Faith Notes

....

....

....

3

Psalm 91:1; Psalm 62:1
DETOX FROM YOUR DIGITAL WORLD

I can't do it," Grace proclaimed. "I'm on my phone all the time. I can't give it up for an entire week!"

I just smiled. No matter how much Grace or any other student argued, I wasn't going to let them bring their phones on this mission trip. "I want you to completely disconnect from your normal routine," I told the group. "We're hooked on technology. This is a once-in-a-lifetime chance to have real freedom and to connect with God in a deeper way."

To date, I've taken more than 1,500 teenagers on trips around the country—all without cell phones. Our adult leaders bring their phones to take photos and use for emergencies, but they stay off their phones as much as possible.

At first, people thought I was nuts for asking students to leave their phones at home. But without exception, as soon as a person went without their phone for a day, their opinion changed.

"I feel free," Grace admitted after the first day without her phone. "I didn't even realize how much time I was spending on my phone. It's like I'm finally seeing the world around me now, without [my phone] being in my hands and demanding my attention all the time."

The world is so fast paced and connected that it's important for us to carve out moments that silence all that noise. In Scripture, we see Jesus' example of inviting the disciples to break away from the crowds and find rest in a place of quiet solitude, where they could pray without distraction and listen to Jesus' lessons for them. In fact, throughout the Bible, we see the men and women of God seeking solace in quiet moments with their heavenly Father. Psalm 91:1 tells us,

> He who dwells in the shelter of the Most High
> will abide in the shadow of the Almighty.

For us, dwelling in the "shelter of the Most High" means disconnecting from the online world so we can better reconnect with ourselves, our God, and the people who mean the most to us. It also means dedicating a portion of our week to participate in a worship service—our shelter from the rest of the world—where Jesus comes to us in Word and Sacrament to renew us, refresh our faith, and strengthen us for the upcoming week.

So—are you up for a digital detox? Are you willing to disconnect in order to nourish your soul?

Even if you can't unplug for a whole week like the students on my mission trips do, try disconnecting for an hour each day. If you need to build up to a full hour, that's okay. However you decide to do it, I encourage you to stash those tempting devices—your phone, smart watch, tablet, video game consoles, and computer—out of sight and to physically separate yourself from them. Consider playing a board game with your friends or family, taking a walk outside, or trying a creative outlet like writing a poem or painting a picture. Psalm 62:1 reminds us,

> For God alone my soul waits in silence;
> from Him comes my salvation.

Let today be the day when you take a break from the busy and find soul-restoring rest with God.

God created a big, wide world for us to enjoy. Live in it and let it recharge you and remind you of God's goodness all around.

Faith Notes

....
....
....
....
....
....
....
....
....
....
....

4

Matthew 5:16

WHAT'S YOUR WITNESS ONLINE?

I read the post again, squinting at the confusing sentiment it expressed.

Despite the Holy Spirit tugging at my heart to reach out to the person who'd posted the cryptic message online, I resisted. *I haven't talked to this person in years,* I argued with myself. *It'll be weird and invasive if I reach out now.*

Yet something about my distant friend's post set off alarm bells. I typed a private message to him that simply said, "Hey, your post has me a little worried. Is there anything I can be praying for you tonight?"

Within a few moments, he responded. He was in a dark place. Incredibly, the Holy Spirit gave me the words to encourage his battered heart and halt his plans of ending his life.

He got help, connecting with a counselor. Eventually, he got past that dark time, got married, and started a family. Now he is happy, healthy, and enjoying his life. I shudder to think about all that he could have missed and the immense pain he would have caused if he had given in to the darkness he was battling.

The digital space has just as many hurting people who need Jesus as the rest of the world. People express their despair online in various ways: depressing posts, rambling videos and stories, and sometimes even threats.

Nearly every teenager I know has had to deal with a friend spiraling online. It can be scary and confusing when you try to help. But sometimes your help is needed. If you see something "off" posted by people you know, don't assume someone else will respond. Reach out and ask if they're okay and how you can pray for them, or offer to point them to a useful resource or trusted adult. If in doubt, bring the issue to an adult who can help you navigate to a helpful response.

As Christians, God calls us to be positive witnesses of our faith in person and online, and this includes caring for the friends on our digital platforms. As Matthew 5:16 tells us,

> In the same way, let your light shine before others, so that they may see your good works and give glory to your Father who is in heaven.

When you engage with others online, use the opportunity to share Christ's forgiveness, love, and hope through your actions and words. Be compassionate and thoughtful in all your interactions. Find ways to share your faith in our Savior, extend encouragement to those who need support, and pray for others.

One of my favorite things to do online is to simply post, "What can I pray for you today?" I'm amazed at how many private messages I get in response from people sharing difficult circumstances.

Our witness online has the potential to impact lives for eternity. Let Christ's love guide you as you navigate the digital world, holding out your faith as a beacon of hope in a dark place.

Faith Notes

....
....
....
....
....
....
....
....
....
....
....
....
....
....
....
....
....
....
....

1

Proverbs 16:9
LET GOD GUIDE YOUR PATH

If you would have asked a five-year-old me what I'd someday be doing as a career, I would have said, "I'll be a famous artist!"

If you'd asked ten-year-old me, I'd have said, "I'll be a cardiologist."

And sixteen-year-old me would have said, "I'll be a lawyer."

Your dreams, like mine, may be diverse and ever-changing. That's because the path to your future meanders as you grow, encounter new people and professions, and experience more life.

It's normal to wonder about what you're meant to do with your life. Will you go to college? Go straight to full-time work after high school? Get married? Have kids? Buy a house in Winnipeg? Become famous for having your own cooking channel? Invent a smoke alarm battery that doesn't suddenly start beeping in the middle of the night?

As Proverbs 16:9 reminds us,

> The heart of man plans his way, but the
> LORD establishes his steps.

While it's good for us to make plans for our lives, God directs our journey. As someone once told me, "Write your plans in pencil, and give God the eraser." His plan for us may not align with what we expect our lives to be, but His way is always better than ours.

When worry about your future starts to make you anxious, remember to connect with God through prayer and worship. Consider the talents and passions He's given you, and reflect on how they might factor into your future. And keep this in mind—your Creator chose you, made you His own child through your Baptism, and placed you where you are at this time in history and at this place in the world. God's plan for you includes acknowledging all He has done and is doing for you, giving Him glory, and serving others. God's plan for you includes sending His Son to live, die, and rise for you.

Ask God to guide your steps as you journey on in life, faithfully preparing for each new adventure with the confidence that comes from knowing God has great plans in store for you.

Faith Notes

....
....
....
....
....
....

2

Matthew 28:18–20
LAST WORDS

My grandma died a few years ago. Her last words, as her nurse sat beside her?

"Am I dying? Oh, good!"

I take comfort knowing that my grandmother loved Jesus. The last time we talked, I played my favorite worship song for her. "I just love songs about Jesus," she told me. "I can't wait to be with Him in heaven."

We pay special attention to last words. Whether they are the last words before someone we love passes away, the conclusive line of a favorite movie, or the closing remarks of a speech, the final words uttered by someone stick in our minds.

Notably, the last words Jesus spoke to His disciples echo the very first words He spoke to them. At the beginning of His ministry, when He called the disciples to follow Him, pulling them away from the mundane routines of their simple lives, Jesus promised that He'd make them fishers of men. In that calling, He gave them an identity and a purpose.

Before Jesus ascended to heaven, after His death and resurrection, He gave the disciples the Great Commission and called them to go forth and make disciples of all nations. Again, He reminded them of their identity and purpose, as we read in Matthew 28:18–20:

> And Jesus came and said to them, "All authority in heaven and on earth has been given to Me. Go therefore and make disciples of all nations, baptizing them in the name of the Father and of the Son and of the Holy Spirit, teaching them to observe all that I have commanded you. And behold, I am with you always, to the end of the age."

With His last words, Jesus reminded the disciples of who they were, what He called them to do, and the fact He was always with them. We do well to remember that Jesus gives us this same promise.

Who are we? We're the baptized, redeemed, forgiven children of God with the hope of eternity stamped on our hearts.

What are we called to do? With faith, given to us by the Holy Spirit, we use the gifts He has given us to give glory to God and share Jesus' grace and the Good News with the weary world around us.

And are we on our own? Never—the Holy Spirit is with us every moment, no matter what we face. Jesus is with us in His Word, in our Baptism, and in the Lord's Supper.

To the very end of the age, our Savior walks beside us. And someday, when I utter my own last words, I hope they reflect the same joy and hope my grandma's final gasp did:

"Am I dying? Oh, good!"

Questions

Who are you, in God's eyes? Speak those words aloud.

Jesus has given you identity as His own beloved, forgiven child. What difference does that make in the way you see yourself?

As Christians, we are called to share the Good News. What gifts and opportunities have you been given that you can use to proclaim this hope to others?

....
....
....
....
....
....
....
....
....
....
....
....
....
....
....
....

3

1 Chronicles 16:11
YOUR CAREER

W hat do you want to be when you grow up?"
How many times do you think you've been asked
that question? Two dozen times? A hundred times?

It's funny that a question people start asking us when
we're tiny is one we continue to be asked through much
of our lives. This question forces us to come up with an
answer, even when we're young and often have no idea
what that career might look like.

Some of my friends have had the same answer since
childhood about what they wanted to be. They always
wanted to be doctors or veterinarians or soldiers. Others
changed their answer frequently, their interests shifting
as they matured. And some people always struggle to
articulate a good answer.

My in-laws still tease Savanna, my husband's youngest
sister, because she used to say she wanted to be a dolphin
when she grew up.

Don't let this question of what you want to do with
your life be a stressor. Even though you may feel pressure
to figure it out and have a good answer, your interests
and passions will unfold and maybe even change over

time. You may try something new and discover that you love it, or you may focus on something only to eventually realize that you don't enjoy it as much as you imagined.

A good verse to guide us as we consider our future is 1 Chronicles 16:11:

> Seek the LORD and His strength; seek
> His presence continually!

The Lord's strength is His power over all things, especially His power over evil and death, which Jesus defeated for us. His presence is in His Word and in the sacraments of Baptism and the Lord's Supper.

Be confident that your Creator gave you one-of-a-kind skills, passions, and interests that make you unique. And He is with you throughout your whole life's journey. He lays a path for you as you make your way through this world, opening and closing doors and seeing new vantage points as you continue to mature. Under His skillful hand, you can confidently walk into the opportunities in front of you.

Tackle each day one step at a time, trusting that God loves you, guides you, and protects you. He alone knows what is best for you, what will challenge and stretch you, and what will form your character. He will be with you on every step of the road.

Journal about the ways He has guided your paths so far. What paths are in front of you now?

4

Psalm 119:105, James 1:5
MAKING DECISIONS

Decisions, decisions. They start as soon as you open your eyes and confront you all day long; sometimes they persist even in your sleep.

What should I wear?

What should I eat for lunch?

Whom should I partner with for the group project?

How do I do this?

What should I say?

Life presents us with a smorgasbord of decisions to make every day. Some decisions are small, but others are complex and carry profound implications. Our future is directly shaped by the decisions we make, however, so it's important that we make the right ones.

But how do we do that?

When making decisions, we should seek God's guidance in His Word and align with His guidelines (the Commandments) for how to live our lives. Scripture is full of advice on how to behave and treat others in ways that will please God, uplift our souls, and benefit the people around us.

By regularly going to God's Word, our decisions can be guided by His truth. As Psalm 119:105 tells us,

Your word is a lamp to my feet and a light to my path.

Take time to pray and seek advice from wise, godly people in your life when making decisions. It may be helpful to keep a journal and take notes as you mull over the choices in front of you. Many people find great value in creating a list of pros and cons involved in the decision. After all, God gave you that wonderful brain of yours—He'll work through it!

Remember that God is always ready to listen as you work through your decision-making process. James 1:5 reminds us,

If any of you lacks wisdom, let him ask God, who gives generously to all without reproach, and it will be given him.

When we seek God in our decisions, He blesses us with His wisdom and guides our next steps.

No matter what decisions you make, take comfort in knowing that God's love for you will never falter. You'll make mistakes, miss opportunities, and choose incorrectly plenty of times over the course of your life. Through it all, God will enfold you in His never-ending grace.

God's decision to show His love for you by sending Jesus for you is the decision that matters most.

Journal a prayer of thanksgiving to God for making that decision!

5

1 Corinthians 7:34
EMBRACING SINGLENESS

How many movies and television shows have the same plot? A young, single woman is successful but aloof. She meets a cute guy who she'd never consider dating until she realizes that she's inexplicably in love. They share their first kiss—against the background of twinkling fairy lights—and she's finally happy.

Sigh.

Real relationships don't neatly evolve over the span of a seventy-minute storyline. And contrary to what the movies may tell you, your life has more purpose than spending all your time and energy finding Mr. Right.

Marriage is good and God pleasing, and singleness is equally good and God pleasing. Both are possible future vocations for you. You may desire or see yourself in either of those situations, and you may end up there. Or you may grow up to be in the opposite circumstance of what you expect. You may never get married, and that's fine. You may get married, young or older, and that's fine too. You may deal with divorce, become a single parent, struggle through infertility, have fifteen kids, or get remarried. Guess what? God will use anything and everything in your story for His glory. That's because God has chosen you to be His own beloved child. Before you were born, He laid out a path that is for His purpose and your benefit. Of course, you will make choices about your life, but because Jesus has reconciled you to God, your heavenly Father will bless your choices that align with His will for you.

Paul reminds us in 1 Corinthians 7:34 that singleness gives us the opportunity to give our full attention to God:

> And the unmarried or betrothed woman is anxious about the things of the Lord, how to be holy in body and spirit.

Singleness gives us the space to grow in relationship with God and to grow personally, as an individual. It allows us the opportunity to understand that our worth is not defined by relationship status but in our God-given identity. Being single is a chance to build a meaningful life by investing in friendships, leaning into your passions and interests, and following God's path for your life.

You are much more than any relationship you may be in or want to have. Your worth doesn't come from being a girlfriend, wife, or mother. It comes from Jesus Christ, who redeemed you and calls you His beloved, a person created with purpose.

A season or a lifetime of being single is purposeful. Trust that God has a special plan for you, and it doesn't have to fit into any mold the world has put in front of you. Your journey is yours and it is in God's hands.

6

Philippians 3:13–14
LET GO AND LOOK AHEAD

A s I write this book, I'm in the process of moving from Texas to Oregon. My days are hectic as I deal with packing boxes and making arrangements with my job, the moving company, and a million other stressful details.

Every time I tape up a box, I'm tempted to look back with regret. It's so hard to move, and it'd be easier to stay put.

But that's not what God has called my family to do at this time in our lives.

Every person's journey is filled with beauty and with choices. Sometimes we find ourselves holding on to things that we should release. Perhaps that's a relationship, a job, an unrealized dream, or an old habit that we need to walk away from.

As one of my students told me, "It's like closing the window blinds even though the view is pretty."

Letting go is never easy, especially when you're attached to something. But just because something is comfortable and familiar doesn't mean it's right.

Like glancing in the rearview mirror and seeing the road behind you, it's important to acknowledge your past and learn from it. That doesn't mean you need to stay there forever though. God has big plans for your future, and He will take care of you on this new adventure.

Paul tells us in Philippians 3:13–14 to keep our foot on the gas and keep moving forward. He writes,

> Brothers, I do not consider that I have made it my own. But one thing I do: forgetting what lies behind and straining forward to what lies ahead, I press on toward the goal for the prize of the upward call of God in Christ Jesus.

It's hard to let go and look ahead, but you can be sure of one thing: our almighty God will steer each of us through some amazing adventures on our way to the prize—heaven with Jesus. You are always safe in His hands.

Activity

Are you struggling to let go? Here are a few things to try:

Give voice to your feelings. It's normal to feel sad or worried when letting go. Give yourself permission to feel all your emotions without self-condemnation. Spend some time talking to God out loud or journaling your feelings.

Focus on the now. Remember that you're choosing to focus on the now, not on the past. Keep an ongoing list of all the exciting possibilities ahead for you and look at it when you feel overwhelmed.

Keep moving forward. Keep looking ahead, not living in the rearview mirror. Remind yourself that endings are new beginnings of undiscovered joys. Letting go leads to growth and new blessings.

Pray for the strength to let go of what's holding you back and the faith to step into the unknown. Just like closing the blinds doesn't erase the beauty outside, letting go doesn't diminish your worth or potential. It's simply a step toward the brighter tomorrow that God has in store for you.

....
....
....
....
....
....
....
....
....
....
....
....
....
....
....
....
....

7

Matthew 6:21
WHAT DO YOU TREASURE?

When I was fifteen, a wildfire broke out in my neighborhood in central Minnesota. As fire fighters raced to contain the flames, the police started evacuating our street.

A police officer banged on our door and told us we had a few minutes to grab what we could and leave the area.

My family and I raced to collect our treasures and load up the car, leaving our house behind. I grabbed my jewelry box, journal, a few special mementos, some photos, and my confirmation Bible.

Thankfully, the wildfire was stopped, and we didn't lose anything. But this experience impacted me, showing me clearly what I treasured most.

It's easy to lose sight of what truly matters. Our lives are busy, and we're pulled in different directions with relationships and responsibilities, pursuits and possessions. Against this chaotic backdrop, it can be difficult to recognize what is actually in our hearts.

Matthew 6:21 reminds us,

For where your treasure is, there your heart will be also.

What we treasure is a reflection of our heart, showing us what holds the most worth in our eyes. It's what we value most, and it's different for each of us. My parents and brother grabbed different items than I did because each of our treasures is made valuable by our individual lives, interests, and experiences.

As you consider what you treasure most, know that God's values and characteristics provide framework for a meaningful life. Here are some of the values He expresses in His Word:

- ☐ Love: In Matthew 22:34–40, Jesus teaches us to love God with all our hearts, minds, and souls and to love our neighbors as ourselves. Love is at the core of God's traits and should be important in our lives too.

- ☐ Integrity: Micah 6:8 tells us to do justice, love kindness, and walk humbly with God. These are qualities of integrity and character.

- ☐ Compassion: Matthew 9:35–38 demonstrates that Jesus has compassion for those in need (including our sinful selves). We also have opportunities to extend compassion, especially when people are hurting.

- ☐ Obedience: James 1:22–25 reminds us about the importance of not only hearing God's Word but also doing it.

- ☐ Good Stewardship: In Genesis 1:28, God entrusted humans with the responsibility of caring for creation. Being good stewards of the environment and our resources matters.

When God's values shape our hearts and we treasure what He treasures, we live our lives in harmony with His plan for us, which is righteousness through Jesus. Let integrity, compassion, obedience, and stewardship permeate your life. Above all, let God's limitless love fill you with a sense of peace and purpose.

Activity

Imagine you have five minutes to grab anything you want to save from your house. What would you take? What would these items indicate that you treasure? Do you feel that these are accurate representations of who you are and what you value?

Discuss it with friends or family members and see what they might guess you'd choose, based on how well they know you and what they observe that you treasure.

....
....
....
....
....
....
....
....
....
....
....

8

Philippians 4:6–7; Matthew 6:25, 27, 32–33

OVERCOMING ANXIETY ABOUT YOUR FUTURE

Stacks of college admission packets filled every corner of my closet, threatening to tumble down every time I reached for a pair of shoes.

I had started looking at colleges as an eighth grader. Fast-forward to senior year of high school, and I had dedicated way too much brain power and closet space to trying to discern my future. To be honest, I felt burned out before I even decided what to do or where to go. I was nervous, anxious, and gripped by fear of making the wrong decision.

Can you relate?

Life can feel overwhelming when thoughts about the future fill you with anxiety. It's tough enough to handle the hardships of growing up. When you add the process of trying to figure out what to do with the rest of your life, it can induce serious panic and worry.

As you shoulder this pressure, don't forget that there's a source of strength available for your anxious mind: the comfort of God's Word. Philippians 4:6–7 tells us,

> Do not be anxious about anything, but in everything by prayer and supplication with thanksgiving let your requests be made known to God. And the peace of God, which surpasses all understanding, will guard your hearts and your minds in Christ Jesus.

This verse became a constant prayer throughout my senior year as I finally chose a university and career. In fact, I put this verse inside my graduation announcements because it was such a meaningful reminder of God's peace in a difficult time.

Anxiety about the unknown is a common affliction. In fact, it's been so common for so long that Jesus talked about it in His Sermon on the Mount:

> Therefore I tell you, do not be anxious about your life, what you will eat or what you will drink, nor about your body, what you will put on. Is not life more than food, and the body more than clothing? . . . And which of you by being anxious can add a single hour to his span of life? (Matthew 6:25, 27)

It's true that the people who heard Jesus say this lived two thousand years ago didn't have the same challenges that we do. But God knew their worries and He knows ours.

> Your heavenly Father knows that you need them all. But seek first the kingdom of God and His righteousness, and all these things will be added to you. (Matthew 6:32–33)

The righteousness of God is ours through Jesus. When you feel like you're being consumed by your fears, remember that God is in control. Turn to Him and unload about your worries and doubts, dreams and hopes. He is always there to listen and comfort, providing direction through His Word.

God cares about your life, and He'll guide you in His perfect timing. As one of my mentors once told me, "God lights the path just in time for you to step out onto it."

When we remember to meet our anxiety with faith in the righteousness of God, our focus can be shifted from worry to thanksgiving. Try jotting down one blessing you're grateful for each day. Present your requests to God and ask the Holy Spirit to give you a tangible sense of peace.

The next time you start to worry about your future, turn to God and pray. Recognize your blessings and remember that the same God who has taken care of you will continue to provide on the journey ahead. You can face the future filled with hope and the confidence of knowing that God's love for you in Jesus is steadfast.

Faith Notes

....
....
....
....
....

9

Ecclesiastes 3:1; Proverbs 19:21; Luke 11:9–10
LIVE RIGHT NOW

D o you ever look forward to something else so much that you forget to live in the now?

It's easy to get wrapped up in the future, thinking about what lies ahead. Maybe you're dying to get to high school, desperate to start college, or killing time until a new job starts.

While it's important to have goals, it's equally important to savor today and find joy in your present circumstances. Ecclesiastes 3:1 tells us,

> For everything there is a season, and a
> time for every matter under heaven.

God saturates each season of our life with its own beauty and purpose. Each day holds unique opportunities for growth and delight. He didn't intend for us to rush ahead, with our minds focused only on the future.

To remind myself to live in the now, I often take a break and get into nature. Feeling the sunshine on my face and hearing the trees rustle are simple pleasures. Watching the squirrels dart around and birds perch on the fence reminds me that God's fingerprints are all around me, throughout His entire creation. Proverbs 19:21 tells us,

> Many are the plans in the mind of a man, but it
> is the purpose of the LORD that will stand.

I often forget that God knows me better than anyone and that He has a plan for each season of my life. While you or I may not know what God has planned for tomorrow, we can hold our dreams and goals loosely and surrender our future to our Maker.

You have probably heard Jesus' words in Luke's Gospel account:

> And I tell you, ask, and it will be given to you; seek, and you
> will find; knock, and it will be opened to you. (Luke 11:9)

This verse is comforting for sure. There's more to Jesus' promise here though. In the next verse, He says:

> For everyone who asks receives, and the
> one who seeks finds, and to the one who
> knocks it will be opened. (Luke 11:10)

God will hear your prayers in Jesus' name. Jesus is our intercessor and our mediator—God hears us because of what Jesus did for us on the cross. So, be encouraged to live today with gratitude, enjoying the blessings it brings to your life. No doubt that God has surrounded you with plenty to enjoy, if you take the time to slow down and look around at all He has given you.

Activity

Make a time line of notable experiences and milestone moments in your life up to this point. Arrange them in order of when they occurred. After penciling them in, spend some time reflecting on how God used each experience to shape you. How did you grow through each milestone? How did one step lead to another and another?

Trust that God will continue to shape and mold you through every future experience you encounter.

....
....
....
....
....
....
....
....
....
....
....
....
....
....
....
....

10

Isaiah 43:19
STARTING SOMETHING NEW

The first time I kayaked, it was miserable.

I struggled to launch the boat from the shore, then dropped my paddle in the water. My legs were muddy as I attempted to steer. My arms ached and the boat didn't move very fast.

But I kept trying. I went out again, and again. Over time, my skills and abilities improved so much that I bought my own kayak.

What started out as a challenge became a great joy, a place where I feel peace and reflect on the beauty of God's creation.

Whenever you try something new, it's usually miserable. Your first workout. Your first presentation in front of a class. Your first day of work. Your first attempt at cooking a meal for yourself. Your first college exam. Your first night away from home.

But you can't experience the real satisfaction and joy of doing something new that will eventually emerge without going through this miserable starting point.

Sometimes we let fear steer us away from tackling something new. We don't want to be embarrassed or admit that we don't know how to do something. We worry what others will think.

And old German proverb goes something like this: "fear makes the wolf bigger than it is."

According to His plan for us, God guides our feet into new, unknown territory as we journey through life. His presence provides us with assurance that He holds us safe in His hands, even if we feel uncertainty at the newness of what lies ahead.

Our God reminds us in Isaiah 43:19,

> Behold, I am doing a new thing; now it springs forth, do you not perceive it? I will make a way in the wilderness and rivers in the desert.

Only God can make safe passages through the wilderness, providing what is life-giving in a place where there is nothing else to nourish us. That's because Jesus went there first. Jesus spent forty days in the wilderness, tempted in every way by the evil one. And Jesus went through the agony of separation from God the Father so we wouldn't have to. That's the safe passage our Lord makes for us.

When you step out to try something new, be emboldened by the truth that the God who makes a way in the wilderness is clearing a beautiful path for you to walk. While the unknown twists and turns ahead may be scary, you can trust that your heavenly Father paves the way and accompanies you through this new experience.

Embrace everything new with confidence, trusting that God's got you.

Faith Notes

....
....
....
....
....
....
....
....
....
....
....
....
....
....
....
....
....
....
....
....
....
....
....
....

11

Ecclesiastes 3:1
MOVING ON

I looked around at all my friends sprawled in the basement at someone's house. It was the last time we'd be together like this.

Or, rather, it was the last time *I* would be with them like this.

I was leaving for college, moving across the country. All my friends had decided to stay in Minnesota to pursue their education, and they seemed to think I was bonkers for going to school in California. Some of them had even questioned me and begged me to stay.

Yet I knew it was time for me to move on, spread my wings, and go on a new adventure. I couldn't explain it to them logically, but I trusted that the Holy Spirit was guiding me and would be with me as I embarked on this next step.

That decision to go to college in California changed the course of my life. It was there that I met my husband, met other lifelong friends, and launched my career. While I have no doubt that God would have worked wonderful things in my life if I had gone to college in

Minnesota like these friends, I'm thankful that I took a leap of faith and ended up where I did.

Our lives are full of decisions, and sometimes we need to move on from a friend or group, a boyfriend, a team or club, a job, a school, or even a habit or routine. It's challenging to leave behind what is familiar.

I learned in a neuroscience class in graduate school that the best thing you can do for your brain is to continuously expose it to new things. Even something as simple as driving home a different route or toweling off in a different pattern is good for your brain.

However, no class or textbook exists that can tell you how to correctly make every decision in your life. Sometimes you're faced with tough decisions, and sometimes the better option is hard to discern. You may even have to choose between two good things.

Yet in our journey through life, God calls us to step out in faith, trusting Him to make His will for us known and to guard us against making decisions that would harm us. Life is a series of seasons, and through all of them, we trust God's timing over our own comfort. As Ecclesiastes 3:1 reminds us,

> For everything there is a season, and a time for every matter under heaven.

Remember the account of Abraham? In Genesis, we read about how he followed God's call and left his homeland to go to a new place. Even though it was difficult, Abraham was obedient, and God blessed him greatly in this new land. And Jesus, true man, was obedient and went to the cross, according to God's will, and fulfilled the promise to save us from sin and the eternal punishment that sin deserves. In the same way, God's direction for us is to worship and praise Him, to draw close to Him in prayer and in reading His Word, to receive His good gifts of forgiveness and grace, and to trust Him to guide us. He goes with us into the unknown, lending us His strength and hope, extending new blessings, and giving us the chance to grow.

Let the assurance of God's good will for you fill you with peace as you navigate the decisions ahead. The next time you need to step into something new, you can walk with confidence, knowing that God walks with you.

Faith Notes

....

....

....

....

....

....

....

....

....

....

....

FIFTY-TWO
BIBLE PASSAGES
FOR YOUR LIFE:

When you need peace:
[Jesus said,] "Peace I leave with you; My peace I give to you. Not as the world gives do I give to you. Let not your hearts be troubled, neither let them be afraid." (JOHN 14:27)

When your heart is broken:
The LORD is near to the broken-hearted and saves the crushed in spirit. (PSALM 34:18)

When you feel alone:
Be strong and courageous. Do not be frightened, and do not be dismayed, for the LORD your God is with you wherever you go. (JOSHUA 1:9)

When you feel angry:
Be angry, and do not sin; ponder in your own hearts on your beds, and be silent. Offer right sacrifices, and put your trust in the LORD. (PSALM 4:4–5)

When talking is getting you into trouble:
Even a fool who keeps silent is considered wise; when he closes his lips, he is deemed intelligent. (PROVERBS 17:28)

When you need guidance about social media:
Let no corrupting talk come out of your mouths, but only such as is good for building up, as fits the occasion, that it may give grace to those who hear. (EPHESIANS 4:29)

When you feel like your sin is too big for God:
But God, being rich in mercy, because of the great love with which He loved us, even when we were dead in our trespasses, made us alive together with Christ—by grace you have been saved. (EPHESIANS 2:4–5)

When you need a new start:
If anyone is in Christ, he is a new creation. The old has passed away; behold, the new has come. (2 CORINTHIANS 5:17)

When you feel anxious:
Do not be anxious about anything, but in everything by prayer and supplication with thanksgiving let your requests be made known to God. And the peace of God, which surpasses all understanding, will guard your hearts and your minds in Christ Jesus. (PHILIPPIANS 4:6–7)

When you are tempted by porn:
Finally, brothers, whatever is true, whatever is honorable, whatever is just, whatever is pure, whatever is lovely, whatever is commendable, if there is any excellence, if there is anything worthy of praise, think about these things. What you have learned and received and heard and seen in me—practice these things, and the God of peace will be with you. (PHILIPPIANS 4:8–9)

When you are deciding what to put into your body:
Do you not know that your body is a temple of the Holy Spirit within you, whom you have from God? You are not your own, for you were bought with a price. So glorify God in your body. (1 CORINTHIANS 6:19–20)

When you wonder if anyone cares about you:
[Jesus said,] "For God so loved the world, that He gave His only Son, that whoever believes in Him should not perish but have eternal life. For God did not send His Son into the world to condemn the world, but in order that the world might be saved through Him." (JOHN 3:16–17)

When you feel overwhelmed:
[Jesus said,] "Come to Me, all who labor and are heavy laden, and I will give you rest." (MATTHEW 11:28)

When you need confidence:
I can do all things through Him who strengthens me. (PHILIPPIANS 4:13)

When you wonder if God is real:
The heavens declare the glory of God, and the sky above proclaims His handiwork. Day to day pours out speech, and night to night reveals knowledge. There is no speech, nor are there words, whose voice is not heard. Their voice goes out through all the earth, and their words to the end of the world. (PSALM 19:1–4)

When you're sad:
Weeping may tarry for the night, but joy comes with the morning. (PSALM 30:5)

When you wonder if you have any talents:
Now there are varieties of gifts, but the same Spirit; and there are varieties of service, but the same Lord; and there are varieties of activities, but it is the same God who empowers them all in everyone. To each is given the manifestation of the Spirit for the common good. (1 CORINTHIANS 12:4–7)

When you wonder if God has a plan for your life:
For I know the plans I have for you, declares the LORD, plans for welfare and not for evil, to give you a future and a hope. (JEREMIAH 29:11)

When you wonder what to do with your troubles:
Cast your burden on the LORD, and He will sustain you; He will never permit the righteous to be moved. (PSALM 55:22)

When you wonder if God listens to you:
Call upon Me in the day of trouble; I will deliver you, and you shall glorify Me. (PSALM 50:15)

When you feel like your hurt is a waste:
As for you, you meant evil against me, but God meant it for good, to bring it about that many people should be kept alive, as they are today. (GENESIS 50:20)

When you feel like life's circumstances are too much for God:
For I am sure that neither death nor life, nor angels nor rulers, nor things present nor things to come, nor powers, nor height nor depth, nor anything else in all creation, will be able to separate us from the love of God in Christ Jesus our Lord. (ROMANS 8:38–39)

When bad news seems to have triumphed:

[Jesus said,] "In the world you will have tribulation. But take heart; I have overcome the world." (JOHN 16:33)

When you need forgiveness:

Come now, let us reason together, says the LORD: though your sins are like scarlet, they shall be as white as snow; though they are red like crimson, they shall become like wool. (ISAIAH 1:18)

When you experience sexual temptation:

For this is the will of God, your sanctification: that you abstain from sexual immorality. (1 THESSALONIANS 4:3)

When you want to live in step with the Holy Spirit:

But the fruit of the Spirit is love, joy, peace, patience, kindness, goodness, faithfulness, gentleness, self-control; against such things there is no law. And those who belong to Christ Jesus have crucified the flesh with its passions and desires. If we live by the Spirit, let us also keep in step with the Spirit. (GALATIANS 5:22–25)

When you want to know the secret to a successful life:

Put on then, as God's chosen ones, holy and beloved, compassionate hearts, kindness, humility, meekness, and patience, bearing with one another and, if one has a complaint against another, forgiving each other; as the Lord has forgiven you, so you also must forgive. And above all these put on love, which binds everything together in perfect harmony. And let the peace of Christ rule in your hearts, to which indeed you were called in one body. And be thankful. Let the word of Christ dwell in you richly, teaching and admonishing one another in all wisdom, singing psalms and hymns and spiritual songs, with thankfulness in your hearts to God. And whatever you do, in word or deed, do everything in the name of the Lord Jesus, giving thanks to God the Father through Him. (COLOSSIANS 3:12–17)

When you need to know how to love someone:

Love is patient and kind; love does not envy or boast; it is not arrogant or rude. It does not insist on its own way; it is not irritable or resentful; it does not rejoice at wrongdoing, but rejoices with the truth. Love bears all things, believes all things, hopes all things, endures all things. Love never ends. (1 CORINTHIANS 13:4–8)

When you're wondering how to treat your parents:

Honor your father and your mother, that your days may be long in the land that the LORD your God is giving you. (EXODUS 20:12)

When you're tempted by drugs or alcohol:

Do not get drunk with wine, for that is debauchery, but be filled with the Spirit. (EPHESIANS 5:18)

When you need to know how to treat other people:

Be kind to one another, tender-hearted, forgiving one another, as God in Christ forgave you. (EPHESIANS 4:32)

When you need to know what Jesus has done for you:

But He was pierced for our transgressions; He was crushed for our iniquities; upon Him was the chastisement that brought us peace, and with His wounds we are healed. (ISAIAH 53:5)

When you need purpose:

I will make you as a light for the nations, that My salvation may reach to the end of the earth. (ISAIAH 49:6)

When you need to know what sin looks like:

[Jesus said,] "For from within, out of the heart of man, come evil thoughts, sexual immorality, theft, murder, adultery, coveting, wickedness, deceit, sensuality, envy, slander, pride, foolishness. All these evil things come from within, and they defile a person." (MARK 7:21–23)

When you need wisdom instead of foolishness:

The way of a fool is right in his own eyes, but a wise man listens to advice. (PROVERBS 12:15)

One who is wise is cautious and turns away from evil, but a fool is reckless and careless. (PROVERBS 14:16)

**When you need to know
how Baptism blesses you:**
But when the goodness and loving
kindness of God our Savior appeared,
He saved us, not because of works
done by us in righteousness, but
according to His own mercy, by the
washing of regeneration and renewal
of the Holy Spirit, whom He poured
out on us richly through Jesus Christ
our Savior, so that being justified by
His grace we might become heirs
according to the hope of eternal life.
(TITUS 3:4–7)

**When you need to know
how Holy Communion
blesses you:**
Jesus took bread, and after blessing it broke it and gave it to the
disciples, and said, "Take, eat; this
is My body." And He took a cup,
and when He had given thanks He
gave it to them, saying, "Drink of
it, all of you, for this is My blood
of the covenant, which is poured
out for many for the forgiveness of
sins." (MATTHEW 26:26–28)

**When you need
strength to endure:**
[Jesus said,] "Be faithful unto death,
and I will give you the crown of life."
(REVELATION 2:10)

**When you think you
need to be perfect:**
But God shows His love for us in that
while we were still sinners, Christ
died for us. (ROMANS 5:8)

**When you don't know
what to pray for:**
Likewise the Spirit helps us in our
weakness. For we do not know what
to pray for as we ought, but the Spirit
Himself intercedes for us with groan-
ings too deep for words. (ROMANS 8:26)

When life is disappointing:
For I consider that the sufferings
of this present time are not worth
comparing with the glory that is to be
revealed to us. (ROMANS 8:18)

**When bad events
seem to win:**
And we know that for those who
love God all things work together
for good, for those who are
called according to His purpose.
(ROMANS 8:28)

When you wonder if other religions or philosophies are better that Christianity:
This Jesus is the stone that was rejected by you, the builders, which has become the cornerstone. And there is salvation in no one else, for there is no other name under heaven given among men by which we must be saved. (ACTS 4:11–12)

When you wonder if you're good enough:
For by grace you have been saved through faith. And this is not your own doing; it is the gift of God, not a result of works, so that no one may boast. For we are His workmanship, created in Christ Jesus for good works, which God prepared beforehand, that we should walk in them. (EPHESIANS 2:8–10)

When you need strength:
I have been crucified with Christ. It is no longer I who live, but Christ who lives in me. And the life I now live in the flesh I live by faith in the Son of God, who loved me and gave Himself for me. (GALATIANS 2:20)

When you need God's guidance:
Your word is a lamp to my feet and a light to my path. (PSALM 119:105)

When you need God's gifts to fight the spiritual battle:
Finally, be strong in the Lord and in the strength of His might. Put on the whole armor of God, that you may be able to stand against the schemes of the devil. For we do not wrestle against flesh and blood, but against the rulers, against the authorities, against the cosmic powers over this present darkness, against the spiritual forces of evil in the heavenly places. Therefore take up the whole armor of God, that you may be able to withstand in the evil day, and having done all, to stand firm. (EPHESIANS 6:10–13) (Read verses 14–18 to see your armor.)

When you feel weak:
But [Jesus] said to me, "My grace is sufficient for you, for My power is made perfect in weakness." Therefore I will boast all the more gladly of my weaknesses, so that the power of Christ may rest upon me. (2 CORINTHIANS 12:9)

When you think your hopes are impossible:
What no eye has seen, nor ear heard, nor the heart of man imagined, what God has prepared for those who love Him. (1 CORINTHIANS 2:9)

When you're ready to give up:
Even youths shall faint and be
weary, and young men shall fall
exhausted; but they who wait for
the LORD shall renew their strength;
they shall mount up with wings like
eagles; they shall run and not be
weary; they shall walk and not faint.
(ISAIAH 40:30–31)

When you need eternal hope:
[Jesus said,] "I am the resurrection
and the life. Whoever believes in Me,
though he die, yet shall he live, and
everyone who lives and believes in
Me shall never die. Do you believe
this?" (JOHN 11:25–26)